As He Is... So Are We

Richard Van Winkle

COMING
GLORY
PRESS

Lewisville, TX

As He Is… So Are We

Copyright © 2018 by Richard Van Winkle

For information contact:
The Shepherd's House Church
225 Milton St.
Lewisville, TX 75057
http://www.tshlewisville.com
https://www.thecominggloryrevival.com/

The author has italicized Scripture quotations.

Quotations by Andrew Murray taken from "Humility" by Andrew Murray Originally published in New York: Anson D. F. Randolph & Co. 1895 Currently in the public domain

Image of Jesus used by permission by Marchiano Ministries. All rights reserved.

ISBN: 0692132325

Third Edition: March, 2019

12 11 10 9 8 7 6 5 4 3

To my loving wife Dorothy, who is my faithful friend and partner in ministry. I can say without hesitation that this book could not have been possible without her constant encouragement and abiding love.

Foreword

It was back in 1994 that I first met Richard Van Winkle. I was traveling back to Scotland and was encouraged to stop off for a night to meet the pastor of The Shepherd's House. It has been a great honor for me to have walked together with him these 24 years. You learn a lot about someone after that length of time -- who they are, their family, their church, and their walk with God. This book comes out of his walk with God and the way he meditates in the Word of God. It is reflected in the way he lives, his love for Jesus and His body, his relationship with his wife Dorothy (now married these 50 years) and in his kids and grandkids.

You can't offend this man! He just refuses to allow anyone to offend him. He will not let anything get in the way of his relationship with God. In my personal opinion, the last chapter of this book holds the key to the revelation God has given to him in every chapter written: *How to Meditate on the Word of God.*

Out of his meditations and time spent with the Lord, he takes you on a journey through the Scriptures, revealing revelation after revelation. He has woven this in grace and humility, and he builds hope into the reader so that they too can have this divine connection (relationship) with the Lord. It is truly a feast at the table of the Lord. No matter how long you have known the Lord, there is something in here for you.

For those of you who are new believers, read it as part of building your foundation in your Christian walk. You will learn to hear God's voice and how to journey with the Lord. It will help shape your character as you seek to grow in the Lord, and the more you read it, the more you will learn. A great way to read it is with someone who is discipling you or in a home group discussion time. You will be able to pull out principles and truth to live by.

If you are in a Bible school, as I know Richard travels and speaks into the Charis Bible Colleges, grab the book because you will never retain all the information as he preaches! He is there to set you up for a great start in your ministry and to help you launch out and be effective wherever God takes you.

This is a resource to help you grow in your relationship with the Holy Spirit. I quote from chapter eleven, *Our Identity in Christ, "Oh, how much He loves us! When we are born again, we become a vital part of His body."* It's important to know that you fit and have a vital part to play as you journey with the Lord.

This book is about a man's journey through the ups and downs of life. It reflects a prayer life of intimacy with the Lord, and many hours of meditation in His Word. Richard's journey can more than help you in your journey as you take the love of Jesus and give it away to the generations to come.

Richard writes in chapter ten that the Lord told him He wanted to use him to bring liberty and freedom to the body of Christ. As life unfolds, we see the need for freedom in Christ like never before. I can assure you that you will find some keys to help you walk in that freedom, grace, humility, and identity in our loving Savior, Jesus Christ.

Thank you, Richard, for your love and commitment to Jesus, your friendship through the years, and for leading the way in writing this book, which will be a resource for many as they seek to grow in their walk with the Lord.

Joseph Ewen

Leader of the River Church Network in the North East of Scotland, and a prophetic voice to the Shepherd's House and the Antioch Church Movement in Waco Texas

Note to the Reader

This book is a compilation of foundational Biblical principles and spiritual insights into the heart of God, presented through a series of sermons by Pastor Richard Van Winkle.

Since sermons are customarily orated and not written, these messages have been edited for better readability; however, the primary content and flow have not been altered. It is our prayer and sincere desire that this book will provide readers with the same insight, revelation, and inspiration it has given those fortunate enough to hear his messages in person.

May the Holy Spirit reveal the very essence of 1 John 4:17 in every aspect of your life, and may you go forth in the fullness and manifested glory of Christ; for as He is, so are *you* in the earth today!

"...as he is, so are we in this world."

1 John 4:17

CONTENTS

CHAPTER ONE

JESUS IS THE FIRSTBORN

For the past few years, I've had the great privilege of teaching at various schools of ministry around the world, imparting the vision of God's glory to the next generation of ministers. After several months of almost non-stop travel, I found myself completing a three-day session at a Bible college in Oklahoma City. Although more than a little travel-weary, I suspected that something very special was on the agenda that day.

The Lord had recently revealed to me that "Jesus is the firstborn of many identical twins" and it was burning within me to share this revelation with the students. It has been my experience that Saturday morning sessions tend to have sparse attendance, so I was not surprised or disappointed by the low turnout. However, a very unusual thing occurred as I began to minister. An increasingly steady stream of people started coming in the room -- almost minute by minute -- throughout the entire session. At one point, the team leader even asked if we could pause for a short break because more chairs were needed to accommodate the growing crowd. I found the expanding group interesting, but what the Holy Spirit was saying and doing in this session was so personally moving that I barely gave them a passing thought.

Later, I was surprised to discover that those in attendance were so encouraged by what they were hearing, they began calling and texting their classmates, friends, and family.

"You've got to come and hear this!"

They were urging them to drop whatever they were doing and come listen to this message.

As the crowd grew, the revelation of "We are His identical twin" increased in the hearts of those students until papers stopped rattling, sidebar comments trailed off, and we abruptly found ourselves assembled in total silence. Everything just stopped, and for a few moments it felt as though time ceased to exist. In awe and reverence, no one uttered a word as we became profoundly aware that the Spirit of the Lord Himself had descended into the room, and onto everyone there.

The weight of His presence was heavy -- almost tangible. In this silent stillness, His Spirit continued to intensify. Then without prompting or leading, the students suddenly began to erupt with prophecies, tongues and interpretations, and words of knowledge and wisdom. This went on for over an hour, like an orchestra being led by an unseen conductor. One by one, the students responded to the leading of the Spirit; releasing life-changing ministry, imparting new gifts and callings, and revealing God's plans and purposes. That day, lives were changed for eternity.

What an astounding truth: *We are His identical twin!* It was an incredible thing to realize, and to then experience the results. Romans 8:29 says,

> *"For those whom he foreknew he also predestined to be conformed to the image of his Son, in order that he might be the first-born among many brethren."*

Now, allow me to fine-tune it a little bit, and I will back it up with Scripture.

> *"For those whom he foreknew, he also predestined to be conformed to the image of his Son, in order that he might be the first-born among... [identical twins]."*

There are several key differences between fraternal and identical twins. Fraternal twins come from two separate eggs, fertilized by two different sperm and each has its own unique DNA. Since fraternal twins originate from separate eggs, the result can be two boys, two girls, or one of each. It is also possible that they can have two different fathers.

Identical twins, however, come from only one father, a single egg, and a single seed. As this fertilized egg splits, two separate but identical babies begin to develop in the mother's womb. They share a blood type and identical DNA. A good friend of ours has an identical twin brother, and I honestly cannot tell them apart.

Mary conceived Jesus by the power of the Holy Spirit when He placed His seed into the egg in Mary's womb. On a spiritual level, Mary conceived Jesus (the Word of God) by the power of the Holy Spirit. He placed the Word, (the Seed, the Living Word, Christ Himself), into Mary's womb, and the Word became flesh and dwelt among us.

"But now that faith has come, we are no longer under a custodian; for in Christ Jesus you are all sons of God, through faith. For as many of you as were baptized into Christ have put on Christ. There is neither Jew nor Greek, there is neither slave nor free, there is neither male nor female; for you are all one in Christ Jesus (Galatians 3:25-28).

Paul is referring to our spirit here. Even though we are physically born male or female, our spirit has no gender. It isn't male or female, black or white, slave or free; we are only one with Jesus Christ.

When we receive Christ and become born again, God places everything of Himself into our spirit, and conception takes place by the Word of God through His Spirit (the seed) which fertilizes our spirit (the egg). As the egg splits, an amazing process begins. Christ starts to form in us: spirit, soul, and body. I use the word *process* here because seeds take time to grow.

And that Christ may dwell in your hearts through faith; that you, being rooted and grounded in love, may have power to comprehend with all the saints what is the breadth and length and height and depth, and to know the love of Christ which surpasses knowledge, that you may be filled with all the fulness of God (Ephesians 3:17-19).

As we mature and yield to this ongoing process, we increasingly develop into His image and likeness. Our spiritual nature conforms and renews our mind. Then, from our spirit, the Holy Spirit and the Word of God work together to heal and transform our physical body, which is the dwelling place of God. The very essence of Jesus works in our mind, soul, and body, as we gradually become exactly as He is.

Understand, though; we could never qualify to be *The Son of God,* the Second Person in the Godhead. Jesus is The Son of God as well as the Son of Man. He is "The Word" who became flesh and dwelt among us, and He came to exemplify how we should live on earth.

In every set of twins, one will always be born first. Therefore, Jesus was the firstborn among many identical twins because we are all born of His Spirit.

"As he is, so are we in this world" (1 John 4:17).

You became identical to Jesus the minute you were born again. You also became one in spirit.

"But he who is united to the Lord becomes one spirit with him" (1 Corinthians 6:17).

Our spirit connects with the world through our physical being, and we are His temple. This means if we don't declare His message, it won't be spoken, and if we don't go, neither does Jesus. We glorify Him with our body, and it belongs to Him. Paul said,

"Do you not know that your body is a temple of the Holy Spirit within you, which you have from God? You are not your own; you were bought with a price. So glorify God in your body" (1 Corinthians 6:19,20).

Your spirit is unified with Jesus. The Holy Spirit and the Word of God work together to renew your mind and produce power and grace in your body, so you won't gravitate to sin anymore. You may not realize it, but sin is dead; it's under your feet!

"You have been born anew, not of perishable seed, but of imperishable, through the living and abiding Word of God" (1 Peter 1:23).

Begin to see yourself as the spitting image of Jesus! As you look in the mirror of faith, you will notice gradual changes taking place. The more you recognize this, the more you will begin to reflect His image. As you allow the Holy Spirit to have His way, other people will also begin to see Jesus in you. However, this can only take place through humility.

"My little children, with whom I am again in travail until Christ be formed in you" (Galatians 4:19).

I'm reminded of when the Lord spoke to me and said,

"You know son, everything in creation obeys me except my children. They are the only ones capable of disobedience. The seas roar, the winds blow, the stars are in position, the animals do what they do..."

Only people rebel against God. He gave us free will, and this means we have freedom of choice. Choose to humble yourself. As you acknowledge how much more you are beginning to resemble Jesus, the more truth and life you will speak into yourself, and you will soon begin to realize who you really are.

Whenever someone recognizes Jesus in me, they are seeing the new man because I am one with Him. I happily receive the compliment because it's a reminder that I'm becoming more like Him in every way. This includes the way I speak, the way I act, and the way I genuinely love people. It proves that Christ is increasing in me as I co-labor with Him, and the Spirit of Grace and the Word of God make it possible.

The finest compliment you will ever receive is hearing someone say that you remind them of Jesus; there is just no higher praise. So, when someone says, "You remind me so much of Jesus," I just say, "Thank you! What a compliment!" False humility would say, "Oh, it's not me, it's the Lord." You may not realize it, but you just denied His work in you and disqualified yourself from being a co-laborer with Christ.

On the other hand, how would you like to hear somebody say you remind them of the devil? That's certainly not a compliment, and it should never be true of us who are born again in the image of Christ. As you allow Him to permeate every part of your being, the greatest privilege you'll ever have will be making the precious name of Jesus known to others. This is our purpose on earth! Jesus asked Philip,

> *"Have I been with you so long, and yet you do not know me, Philip? He who has seen me has seen the Father... "* (John 14:9).

I strive to be conformed to His image and likeness as much as possible in this life. I may not have a resurrected body yet, but I have the *power* of a resurrected body living in me! We are the fragrance and reflection of the Lord Jesus Christ.

CHAPTER TWO

SUPERNATURAL GROWTH

L ET'S TALK ABOUT GROWTH. There is physical growth, spiritual growth, and then there is *supernatural* growth, and laws govern each of them.

"For the law of the Spirit of life in Christ Jesus has set me free from the law of sin and death" (Romans 8:2).

Physical growth began taking place at the very moment of conception. It was automatic. You didn't have to think about it; it just happened. As you grew, development was predictable, and you gradually progressed through various stages into adulthood. It was a natural process. Jesus said you can't add one cubic inch to your height by thinking about it. It doesn't matter whether you're five or six feet tall; wishing will never change how tall you will be. It will just happen because it's in your genes, and it's who you are.

There are laws of physical growth. If you eat right, drink water, and practice healthy habits, physical growth will naturally take place. Then again, you can do other things which will hinder or stop your physical growth altogether. If you stop eating or drinking water or decide to put unhealthy substances into your body or put a plastic bag over your head, your physical growth and health will suffer. But under ordinary circumstances, physical growth just happens because of natural physical laws.

The same principles apply to spiritual growth. The Holy Spirit's purpose is to help us grow and evolve into the image of the Lord Jesus Christ. When we live by the laws of the Spirit, it's also an automatic process, and will just naturally occur.

If Adam were standing here and Jesus was standing over there, which would be greater? This isn't a tough question. We know that Jesus is infinitely superior to Adam! Adam represents our old nature, and Jesus exemplifies our new one. So, which is greater, your old nature or your new one? The answer is obvious. We need to wake up and put on the new man every day.

Our biggest problem is that most of us pay a lot more attention to our old man than the new one. Why in the world would we do this, knowing the new man is so much greater? Christ is worthy, and Adam is not. There is no way to even compare the two. God is so much greater, and as a new creation, *I* am far greater than the old man who is dead and gone.

This isn't hard to grasp, but our self-will can get in the way. We don't have a sin problem; we have a *SELF* problem. Resisting the new man's thinking and actions will always hinder our spiritual growth. When we are wrapped up in ourselves, we quench the Spirit because He can't operate in us under those conditions.

One thing that affects our spiritual growth is *how* we listen when we hear the Word. We must always listen for ourselves, instead of for somebody else.

"Well, that person really needs to hear this, Lord!"

Whenever we listen for someone else instead of for ourselves, we don't understand that none of us have arrived, and we all have so much room for growth. Greater is He that is in you now than the old man who used to be there! We must know how to put on the Lord Jesus Christ and walk in the new man, and I'm going to show you how.

If you were seriously ill and someone handed you a pill, claiming it would instantly cure everything you've got, you'd be foolish not take it, right? If it worked, you would run around telling everybody, "Hey! I've found something amazing, and when you take it, you're going to get well!"

The good news is Jesus is already in you, and He will make you well. His Word is in us, and as we receive God's Word with meekness, it grows because it is an incorruptible seed. The Holy Spirit waters and activates it inside of us, and as a result, we mature into a mirror image of Jesus. This is an incredible truth, and humility is the key. Scripture tells us that a man *is* as he thinks in his heart, and

> "Out of the abundance of the mouth, the heart speaks"
> (Luke 6:45).

Your heart will automatically produce whatever you plant there. If you're sowing more of the world into your heart than the Word, the world will rule your life instead of the new man. All of God grows out of the soil of humility because Jesus was the Humble One and is our example of humility.

Have this mind among yourselves, which is yours in Christ Jesus, who, though he was in the form of God, did not count equality with God a thing to be grasped, but emptied himself, taking the form of a servant, being born in the likeness of men. And being found in human form he humbled himself and became obedient unto death, even death on a cross (Philippians 2:5-8).

Lucifer exalted himself and declared he would ascend above God because of pride. Then he appealed to Adam's pride in the garden by sowing seeds of temptation, and when Adam bought into Satan's lies, he died spiritually and sowed the seeds of death. Sin entered the world through the first Adam, but Christ came and brought humility back to man. Now His Spirit is in us, and He doesn't change.

Spiritual growth works like physical growth and automatically takes place by the Spirit and the Word. It instinctively happens because of God's seed in us. It has a purpose and a destiny, and it will grow.

You may think, "I know I *should* get in the Word…" No, you need to get the Word in *you* because once you taste the Word, you will see that the Lord is good. This Word is growing in me, and it's the incorruptible seed I'm born of. I love who I am in Christ! I don't read the Bible for knowledge or information anymore; I read it for transformation by the Holy Ghost.

Humility is death to self and life to the new nature of Christ. Grace, faith, and love grow out of the soil of humility, where there is selflessness. Scripture says to lay aside the sin and weights which so easily beset us *(Hebrews 12:1).* We can only do this through humility. We can attribute all sin and all weights in our life to a *lack* of humility, and we cannot lay them aside without Jesus. Supernatural growth spontaneously takes place when we are humble, and humility means that I believe *everything* God says.

"Let it be to me according to your word" (Luke 1:38).

I don't place my value on what people think of me; I only set my value on what God thinks of me. Don't place your value on what your friends think, because the Bible says corrupt friends will corrupt you *(1 Corinthians 15:33)*. Instead, put your value on the Lord's opinion of you, and on who He says you are.

I had to leave my friends. Which friends? My "great" friends who got me drunk, got me in fights and nearly got me killed on several occasions. I thought they were my good friends at the time, but they were corrupt friends, and I had to separate myself from them. Before long, they came and asked,

"What's wrong with you?"

"I don't do that anymore."

"Do you think you're better than us?"

"No, I don't think I'm better than you, I just don't want to do that stuff anymore."

I tried compromising with them, but I just ended up being a drunk again. Those "friends" were hindering my spiritual growth. You need to understand that you cannot compromise because *whatever you compromise to keep, you will lose*. When you compromise your spiritual growth, you can't expect the Holy Spirit to mature you into the image of Christ.

But guess what? A lot of those old friends of mine wound up saved and even Spirit-filled. One good buddy that I used to party with also became a pastor, and now we don't party the way we used to. These days, we have a great time partying with the Spirit of God.

Like physical growth, the things you do will either benefit or hinder your spiritual growth. If you ignore the laws which keep you spiritually alive and healthy, you will ruin your spiritual growth.

The number one spiritual law that releases every bit of God into your life is humility. Jesus demonstrated His by saying,

> *"Father, if thou art willing, remove this cup from me; nevertheless not my will, but thine, be done" (Luke 22:42).*

Jesus only listened to and emulated His Father. He spent time with the Father every day, and we are to follow His example. It's easy to spot those who spend time with the Lord, just by the way they act. If you're humble before God, it doesn't mean a whole lot to me. But the humility you display toward your brothers and sisters tells me whether you've met with Jesus, or not. How much do you resemble Jesus? Do you gripe, complain, and bellyache? That's the old man. Do you do all things without grumbling and complaining? That's the new man.

Supernatural spiritual growth will take place when we obey the laws of growth, and it starts with humility. In fact, it stays with humility forever. This supernatural growth can abound in your mind, in your thinking, and in your actions to the extent that you become so full of the Holy Spirit that sin, sickness, and disease cannot survive in your body anymore. It becomes impervious to all of those things. This is the goodness of God.

On the other hand, pride will always resist God, and this is the old man rearing his head. The Bible says that the old man is *unable* to submit to God. That's why the Holy Spirit had to put him on the cross and crucify him. Now, I'm alive unto God in Christ Jesus, as a brand-new creation. Things of the old man have passed away, but I must consent for the Lord to grow me supernaturally.

When I was five years old, I didn't think about growing; it just happened. When you have a meal, your body digests the food and sends it into your blood system to nourish you. You understand the process, but you don't consciously think about what the food is doing every time you eat. You don't say, "This tastes good. Now I'm swallowing, and this food is going down to my stomach. Now my stomach juices are digesting it, and it's going into my bloodstream." Of course not! You don't think about it; you just enjoy it.

Spiritually, I don't have to think about the transformation that's taking place either, because it's happening automatically. My thinking, my actions, and my personality are gradually adjusting to the image of Christ.

I used to be an angry young man. I was mad at the world, but that angry young man is dead now. However, he will inevitably try to creep up again if I don't guard against it. When I put on the new man he can't come back around because I'm too busy thinking about new things, and I just don't have time for him anymore.

I will never be able to change myself into the image of Christ. It won't work, because then it becomes self-labors and self-righteousness, which will only put me into bondage. But when I sit back and allow the Spirit to work in me, it's automatic, and it happens naturally. It's one reason I love God's Word. It's the reason I love you. It's the reason I love humanity, and it's the reason I love God; because He's doing the work in me, as the new man agrees with Him. It's not me.

If you are beating yourself up right now, thinking of all the things you *should* be doing, you haven't realized yet that you can't do it in your own strength. You will never be able to make yourself like Jesus. It's impossible and only works as you yield and willingly receive everything He died to give you. Jesus does the changing for you.

This is the Blood Covenant of Jesus. It is so powerful!

Now may the God of peace who brought again from the dead our Lord Jesus, the great shepherd of the sheep, by the blood of the eternal covenant, equip you with everything good that you may do his will, working in you that which is pleasing in his sight, through Jesus Christ; to whom be glory for ever and ever. Amen (Hebrews 13:20, 21).

This describes what God will do in your life because of this Blood Covenant with us. Notice you don't have to do anything, except receive it. It is what the blood of Jesus bought, and it's yours! This is what humility is all about. You see, the old man is full of condemnation and shame, and he can struggle with pride and lust because he is only about himself.

Thankfully, 2 Corinthians 5:17 says the old things have passed away, all things have become new; and all those new things come from God. I don't know about you, but I want to abide in what's new; and it supernaturally takes place in my life. The evidence of this will be how much of Christ others can see in me.

How much of Christ can you detect in my words, and in what I do? I don't need to be in charge anymore, and I don't have to have the last word. In fact, I don't feel compelled to say anything. Sometimes we're so busy talking that we're not listening to God. There are times we just need to be still and quiet, and just remember that He is God.

"...He equips you with everything good that you may do His will" (Hebrews 13:21).

It's impossible to figure out the will of God for my life on my own, but as I read the Word and meditate on it, He has promised to equip me with everything I need to do His will. The Amplified Bible says,

> Now may the God of peace [the source of serenity and spiritual well-being] who brought up from the dead our Lord Jesus, the great Shepherd of the sheep, through the blood that sealed and ratified the eternal covenant, equip you with every good thing to carry out His will and strengthen you [making you complete and perfect as you ought to be], accomplishing in us that which is pleasing in His sight, through Jesus Christ, to whom be the glory forever and ever. Amen (Hebrews 13:20, 21).

If God calls me to do something, it's up to Him to make it happen; not me. He will never tell me to do something, and then expect me to do it my own strength. That would be self-righteousness and reverting to the law, so I will let Him do it, instead. I believe our building is paid off, along with everything else, because God told me to buy it, and wherever He guides He provides. I never pray over the finances of The Shepherd's House because I believe I'm in the will of God, so it's up to Him take care of everything financially.

Most pastors I talk to are dealing with financial issues in their church. It's obvious they're trying to do things in their own strength. I've heard the prayers, "Oh God, we need this! Oh God, we need that!" and I think, "Just stop it!" I don't say it, but sometimes I want to. If they ask my advice, I'll try to correct them with the Word of God.

"Listen, Brother, has God told you to do this?"

"Well, yes."

"Then it's up to Him to pay for it. It's up to Him. Did God tell you to buy that piece of property?

"Well, yes, He did."

"Then why are you begging Him? If He said to buy it, He's
got to give you the money to buy it, and here's the key; if
He doesn't give you the money, *it wasn't God.*"

I know many pastors who have done things in their own
strength. They say, "Oh, God told me to buy that property,"
and they go into debt and then pretty soon they're standing in the
pulpit saying, "You people don't give enough. We've got to pay
for this!" The problem is, they missed God.

God's will for you is to allow the Blood Covenant He made
through His Son to do what He wants to do in your life, and it's
His good pleasure. So, if God has told you to do something, you
can rest assured that He will equip you with everything you will
need to get it done. This even refers to your personality! How
easy is that? Just read these Scriptures and say, "Thank you for
equipping me with your will, and everything I will need to do
it."

The second part of that verse tells us that He's working in you
that which is pleasing in His sight, through Jesus Christ --
forever and ever. The Father works everything in us by His
Word and His Spirit, through His Son, Jesus. When Jesus said it
was finished, it was finished! Now, by the Blood Covenant, God
can work in me whatever is pleasing to Him. I certainly can't
work it in myself; and if I try to, I'll become self-righteous. I'll
think I'm better than everybody else and I'll live by *do's* and
don'ts. The law is comprised of dos and don'ts. Now, I only live
by dos. If I 'do,' I won't 'don't.'

If you're busy reminding God that you *don't* do this, or you
don't do that, stop thinking that way. That's your flesh talking.
Say instead, "I am in the will of God; therefore, God is working

in me what is pleasing in His sight. He's making me like Himself. He's doing the work, and it's not me. I'll choose to be humble enough to let Him do it." You can count on God to equip you with whatever He has called you to do to make you like His Son.

> *May the God of peace himself sanctify you wholly; and may your spirit and soul and body be kept sound and blameless at the coming of our Lord Jesus Christ. He who calls you is faithful, and he will do it (1 Thessalonians 5:23, 24).*

This tells us what God Himself will do. He who calls you is faithful, and you can count on Him to do it. Notice it doesn't say, "He who is faithful called you, and *you* will do it." No, He has called you, and He will do it for you. All you need to do is humble yourself and agree with Him by saying "yes." It's that simple.

However, it's also the toughest thing in the world for many people because self gets in the way. They say, "By golly, I'm going to do what I want to do, and I want to do it myself, and I want to do it my way." They don't realize that when they chose to do whatever *they* wanted to do, they told the Holy Spirit that He can't supernaturally make them grow anymore. They halted the Spirit of Grace working in their lives, as well as their spiritual growth. It's like deciding not to eat another bite of food and shortening their physical lives.

We can't heal ourselves. We can't help ourselves. We can't change ourselves, but we *can* yield and allow God to do it for us. You see, if He left me to spiritually mature in my own strength, I would mess it up. I don't know about you, but I would do an outstanding job of messing things up. But if I let Him do the work in me, it's automatic because He's always faithful.

There have been times when I've gone to bed at night feeling miserable after all hell had broken loose earlier in the day. Have you ever had days like that? I remember one night I went to bed feeling so heavy and sighed, "Jesus, I love you" as I fell asleep. When I woke up the next morning, all the heaviness was gone, and I felt so happy that I got up dancing. It was supernatural, and it was something I could never have done in my own strength.

I want the Lord to do what only He can do and lavish me with everything Jesus suffered for me to have. I want all the grace, all the love, all the faith, all His Word, and all of Himself that He wants to give me -- and He wants me to have everything! His thoughts are greater toward me than the sands of the sea, and every one of them is for a future and a hope and a purpose to make me like His Son. Why anyone would resist Him is beyond me, but it's only out of self-righteousness and pride.

You may think, "I'm not going to humble myself before anybody." Really? Well then, go ahead and live in your pride. But realize that when you get offended, it's about *you*. When things come against you, and you get mad and upset and discouraged, it's about *you*. However, I won't give in to that thinking anymore. I will say, "No! I refuse to feel discouraged because God has put something powerful inside of me. I refuse to give up on God, and I refuse to act in my flesh and give that old dead man control again."

So then, my dear ones, just as you have always obeyed [my instructions with enthusiasm], not only in my presence but now much more in my absence, continue to work out your salvation [that is, cultivate it, bring it to full effect, actively pursue spiritual maturity] with awe-inspired fear and trembling [using serious caution and critical self-evaluation to avoid anything that might offend God or discredit the name of Christ]. For it is [not your strength, but it is] God

who is effectively at work in you, both to will and to work
[that is, strengthening, energizing, and creating in you the
longing and the ability to fulfill your purpose] for His good
pleasure (Philippians 2:12,13). (Amp)

Philippians 2:12 says to work out your own salvation with
fear and trembling. This means I fear God, and I tremble at the
thought of not doing His will. It also sounds like I'm supposed to
work out my own salvation here, but the Amplified clearly
explains that it is *God* working in us; to will and to work,
strengthen, energize, and create in us the longing and ability to
fulfill our purpose for His good pleasure. So, we are not doing
the work; *God is working in us!* It's supernatural growth! He
even gives us the will and the desire to obey Him.

Somebody said Christianity is a lot like a boss who calls to
give you a job and then does all the work for you. All you need
to do is show up and say, "Here I am!"

Now, does this mean you don't need to do anything? No. Paul
said,

"...*I worked harder than any of them, though it was not I,*
but the grace of God which is with me" (1 Corinthians
15:10).

Paul walked ten thousand miles in his lifetime, which didn't
even include his sea voyages. He didn't do all of that walking in
his own strength but was able to do it by the grace of God
working in him.

You don't have to tell babies to grow. Just feed them, and
when they're teenagers, they'll eat you out of house and home
because their bodies are exploding. As we get older, our bodies
slow down, and we don't need to eat like we did when we were
teenagers. I can't eat the way I did when I was that age, or I'd

weigh 500 pounds. I could eat and eat and eat.

Spiritually, it's the same way. You can get yourself to such an extraordinary place that God's spiritual power works through you and conforms you to His image. It just takes off and goes, and you must run to catch up with God on the inside of you. If you have ever run marathons or played sports, you know about acquiring a second wind. Suddenly, your adrenaline kicks in and takes you to the next level. It's like a rocket; and when the second stage hits, it zooms off!

You may feel like your spiritual growth is slow right now, but if you will allow your heart to become a seed of humility and stop talking about yourself and stop thinking about yourself and stop feeling sorry for yourself, you will acquire that second wind, or hit that second stage and take off like a rocket.

Start magnifying God and say, "Thank you, Father, for equipping me with everything I need to do your will. You have even promised to make sure I'm in your will." You will soon notice that you're growing and changing, as a result. One day your iPhone and your favorite TV program won't be as important as God's Word, and you will prefer to be still and spend time in His presence.

He will work these things into you if you'll only allow it and humbling yourself is the key. I've learned the hard way that the other side of the fence and the old man were bad news, but this side is great! I love being filled with God. It's the greatest thing that could ever happen to anyone.

CHAPTER THREE

JESUS CAME TO SERVE

But Jesus called them to him and said, "You know that the rulers of the Gentiles lord it over them, and their great men exercise authority over them. It shall not be so among you; but whoever would be great among you must be your servant, and whoever would be first among you must be your slave; even as the Son of man came not to be served but to serve, and to give his life as a ransom for many" (Matthew 20:25-28).

JESUS CAME IN HUMILITY, not to be served, but instead to serve others. He gave all of Himself so that we can offer all of ourselves back to Him in return. As a result, we can become everything He has called us to be. If I'm going to look to Jesus as the author and finisher of my faith, this is the standard I'm measured by. It pleases God to watch us grow in stature into the fullness of His Son. He loves it! The more of Jesus He can see in us, the happier He gets. The Blood of the Lamb was an extraordinary price to pay for our freedom, and it breaks God's heart to see His children still in needless bondage after we have been liberated.

As I continue to yield in every area of my life, I will steadily be forged into His image and likeness and will overflow with grace. He will fill me with Himself, and everything in me will gradually become identical to Jesus.

> *Now he told a parable to those who were invited, when he marked how they chose the places of honor, saying to them, "When you are invited by anyone to a marriage feast, do not sit down in a place of honor, lest a more eminent man than you be invited by him; and he who invited you both will come and say to you, 'Give place to this man,' and then you will begin with shame to take the lowest place. But when you are invited, go and sit in the lowest place, so that when your host comes he may say to you, 'Friend, go up higher'; then you will be honored in the presence of all who sit at the table with you. For every one who exalts himself will be humbled, and he who humbles himself will be exalted" (Luke 14:7-11).*

Some of you may think, "Oh, now I know how to be the greatest; I will just be humble." Do you recognize your goal is still to be the greatest? If your goal is to be the greatest, there is not an ounce of humility in you. Jesus became humble so that we could do it, too. I want to be like Jesus, and He has enabled me to do it, but I must humble myself and allow Him to exalt me. If I try to promote myself, it won't work. This verse describes what we will look like when we have the heart of Jesus.

> *Therefore, since we are surrounded by so great a cloud of witnesses, let us also lay aside every weight, and sin which clings so closely, and let us run with perseverance*

*the race that is set before us, looking to Jesus the
pioneer and perfecter of our faith, who for the joy that
was set before him endured the cross, despising the
shame, and is seated at the right hand of the throne of
God (Hebrews 12:1,2).*

Look in the mirror. You are His joy! His joy is *you*! Jesus
endured the cross and despised the shame, so we could become
children of His Father and to bring us out of the kingdom of
darkness and into the kingdom of light. He bought our freedom
and our access to the kingdom of God. Jesus was able to suffer
the shame of the cross because He was looking ahead to the joy
He would experience watching us live in freedom and then
seeing us in Heaven. He purchased us with His own blood, and
He did it willingly. However, it was also His Father's plan.

"It was the will of Father to bruise him" (Isaiah 53:10).

It pleased the Father to bruise Him because He loved us that
much. He wanted to save us from the kingdom of darkness and
from hell, which He created for Satan and his followers. How
can we not surrender every part of ourselves in gratitude and
allow the wonderful Holy Spirit of God to possess us, kick the
rest of the old man out, and then fill us with the new man?

It will always be obvious when someone is walking in true
humility. If they no longer feel the need to "have their say," this
is one sign of humility. If they are quietly humble, people will
recognize it. Live and be like Jesus and the world will realize He
is the one who possesses you. We are called to be just like Him.
Since we have the same Spirit and are conforming to His image
and likeness, we should be able to see everything in ourselves
that we see in Jesus.

Sadly, many in the church are primarily after the power they receive from the Holy Spirit. You can receive power and still be an idiot. I know that isn't nice, but it's true. The church at Corinth was the most carnal church there was, yet they walked in great power. Paul said they weren't behind in any gift. They had the power, but they lacked love, which is the most vital element. Paul showed them how to use their power in love, which is pure humility. If we become permeated with God and saturated with humility, all the power God wishes to exert on earth will flow through us because our pride won't be able to mess it up. Jesus said,

> *"For which is the greater, one who sits at the table, or one who serves? Is it not the one who sits at the table? But I am among you as one who serves" (Luke 22:27).*

He was saying, *"Am I not the one who sits at the table? Am I not the King? I am, but I am now among you as one who serves."* As Jesus washed their feet, He was conveying to them that He came as a servant. The Son of God knew who He was, and knew where He was going, yet He took a towel and girded Himself as a servant and washed the feet of man. Then He instructed His disciples to follow this example. It is our example, too. We must see ourselves as one who serves; not as one who is entitled to be served.

Self has no desire to serve, except for its own purposes. Self will serve, but the bottom line is, "What will I get out of it? I will serve you because I want you to bless me." The old self may act humble, but there is usually a hidden motive which asks, "How will this benefit me?"

But when we are dead in Christ and alive in Christ, we will be like Jesus, and our attitude will be, "It's not about me; I'm here to serve." I know who I am in Christ. Jesus came to serve, and yet He is the King of kings, and the Son of the Most High God, but He came to serve those who God created. I'm here to serve you the same way He did; to wash your feet with love, as your servant. There is no guarantee of anything coming back to me because my motive is not to receive anything. My entire life is about giving.

Saint Seraphim of Sarov was a Russian monk who probably knew God better than most of us. His most recognized quotation is, "Acquire a peaceful spirit, and thousands around you will be saved." He lived a solitary life for many years in a monastery. When he left the monastery, the Lord told him to receive people, and hundreds of people came to see him each day for the last ten years of his life. He operated in the gifts of healing and a word of knowledge. As each person came to him, he would fall before them and say, "Christ has risen!" Then he would take their hands and kiss them, and say, "My joy!" Then he would stand up, and tell each person where they came from, and why they came there. Then he healed them. He ministered to tens of thousands of people during this ten-year period.

If you are not walking in humility but want the gifts of the Spirit to flow, it will rapidly become about *you* and how anointed *you* are. We must always keep in mind that healing is a gift of the Holy Spirit, and we are merely the vessels He uses to heal others. You will never be able to heal others in your own power, no matter how anointed you are. If you don't understand this, your gift will become your identity, and then you'll walk in pride. But when you humble yourself to be a servant of all, there will be no limit to what God can do through you.

He will continue to keep our old man on the cross, so His Spirit can occupy our whole being. Then the great mission God called us to will begin to work through us. We will never know how great an impact we could have on this world unless we completely surrender ourselves to God.

The Blood of the Lamb obtained every good thing for us, and

Jesus has given us all of Himself. He's the eternal Lamb of God who lives in us, and He continues to provide more and more grace. All of God, all His love, all His grace, all His power... Everything of God grows out of the soil of humility.

God completed everything, and He has lovingly embedded the grace of humility in you. Just say, "yes!" and get the old man out, because God opposes the proud and gives grace to the humble. When people continually complain, "Somebody did this to me..." or "Somebody did that...," this is nothing but pride. Years ago, the Lord spoke to me and said,

> *"Don't you ever judge my church. You wash her with the water of the Word. It's not your business to change her; it's mine. Be my church then you'll help my church."*

If you want to know how much Jesus *is not* controlling your life, take note of how much the things other people have said or done affect you today. If they still pack an emotional punch, it's because of your pride. I know this sounds challenging, but it's true. When I become full of humility, whatever anyone says or does to me will not affect my relationship with Jesus or with other people. I won't allow someone who is working in the flesh to pull me into the flesh with them. I'm going to stay full of Jesus.

Unfortunately, there will always be someone out there who will try to hurt you. Jesus said it's impossible to avoid tribulation and offenses, but He also added that we don't have to fall victim to them, for we're *in* the world, but not *of* it. Humility gives me the grace to not allow others to upset me to the degree that it affects my walk with Jesus or my love for people. Only humility can keep this grace working in me.

I can choose not to get upset now, and when I do, it doesn't last very long. Circumstances no longer rule me. We have all dealt with difficult situations. I can usually tell when someone is enduring something in their own strength because they lose their joy, which was obviously based on circumstances. This stems from self.

However, when I'm full of God, I don't have to bear anything in my own strength, no matter what comes against me. I accept that Jesus bore it for me, and I allow Him to deal with those situations. I like not being upset most of the time. I used to be upset all the time, to such an extent that I tried to commit suicide. Thank God, He delivered me from that kind of thinking!

Christ not only clothes us with His humility but also with the totality of who He is. We cloak ourselves in His very nature, and He helps us by interceding for us in heaven. Then the Holy Spirit brings the intercessory prayers of Christ to earth and manifests them in our lives.

> *Likewise the Spirit helps us in our weakness; for we do not know how to pray as we ought, but the Spirit himself intercedes for us with sighs too deep for words* (*Romans 8:26*).

The new man loves being humble, but the old man will always enjoy being humble only to the extent he's still being acknowledged. The new man lives in such humility that it's no longer us who live, but Christ living in us. When you humble yourself enough to allow God to fill you with Himself, you will discover that you're just like Jesus; and you can't do this through condemnation or by any effort of your own.

God wants His kingdom in your life so that He will be recognized in you. The resulting power will be beyond belief because of your humility. Christ lives in us and increasingly manifests His will for us as we become more like Him, our perfect example.

"It is no longer I who live, but Christ who lives in me" *(Galatians 2:20).*

CHAPTER FOUR

IT TAKES HUMILITY TO BELIEVE

GOD HAS PRESENTED US with a new identity in Christ and has said so many amazing things about us, but we must humble ourselves to believe them. Only grace gives us the ability to do this. God is not a man that He should lie. If we don't accept one hundred percent of what He has said about us, we are walking in pride because we will more readily accept our own opinion or even the view of others, above God's. Therefore, we must humble ourselves and say, "God, you are never wrong. Whatever you say about me is true, so please give me the grace to believe it." Most people cannot even begin to grasp the concept of humility because it is so contradictory to the old man's nature.

Pride guarantees that we will resist God. In fact, when we do our own thing and walk in self and pride, it suppresses our sensitivity to God and deadens everything in us which belongs to Him. Self is the problem and self will always oppose humility. When I give control to self, I'm functioning in sin, and I'm missing the mark.

Humility accepts that I am a new creation, and the things of the old man have passed away. God will continue to eradicate our flesh, so His Spirit can occupy our whole being. As a result, the divine purpose God has called us to will become clear in our lives. In the kingdom of God, the Spirit of Humility is to be the servant of all.

If you have areas in your life where things aren't functioning correctly, where you're frustrated, or where you don't know what God is doing, look for a lack of humility. The old man cannot submit to God, so the Holy Spirit had to put him on the cross and crucify him. Pride is also responsible for the development of our own doctrines and personal philosophies which have nothing to do with the gospel of Jesus Christ. Without humility, it is not only impossible to accept what God says about us but also ensures that we will resist the Holy Spirit as He begins to make necessary changes in our lives.

Humility changes us for a higher purpose and welcomes our transformation into the image of Christ. It allows God to develop in us the mind of Christ to become all that He is. This will enable us to fulfill His will and purpose in our lives. Humility also allows me to consider what God says over anything the world says, or what other people say. I won't even listen to what I say about myself if it doesn't agree with God.

Jesus said His sheep would know His voice and they would not entertain the voice of strangers. The voice of strangers is self. One of the first things you must do after getting saved is to accept that Jesus is your Shepherd and you're the sheep. In over forty-five years of ministry, I've heard many Christians declare they can't hear God's voice. The reason they can't hear God is because pride is getting in the way. Jesus said,

> *To him the gatekeeper opens; the sheep hear his voice, and*
> *he calls his own sheep by name and leads them out. When*
> *he has brought out all his own, he goes before them, and the*
> *sheep follow him, for they know his voice. A stranger they*
> *will not follow, but they will flee from him, for they do not*
> *know the voice of strangers (John 10:3-5).*

If you believe you can't hear the voice of God, you deny the truth that Jesus is your Shepherd, and you can hear His voice. If you think you are an exception, and this Scripture doesn't apply to you, this is pride talking. When I began serving the Lord, I took John 10:4 and I read it out loud. I said over and over and over, "Jesus, I do hear your voice, and I don't entertain the voice of a stranger. Thank you--You're my Shepherd! I am your sheep, and I hear your voice."

It wasn't long before I began to hear God's voice! I started to recognize the voice of my Shepherd, and I also learned to discern when it was the voice of a stranger, the enemy, or the flesh, and not God Himself. If you want to hear the voice of God, say, "Lord, you know I'm having a hard time hearing your voice, but you have said that you're my Shepherd and I'm your sheep, and I do hear your voice. Thank You, Jesus!" Then you listen and say it again and again until you finally do hear and recognize His voice. You will discover His voice is leading you and you will be able to discern it from the voice of strangers. You can't hear the voice of God in your own being; you can only hear it through humility and grace.

When I walk in humility, I embrace grace. I won't focus on what people think of me but will put my value in what God thinks of me, and He thinks I'm pretty special. He says we're His children. Have you ever proudly displayed pictures of your children or grandchildren? If we love our family this way, how much more does God love us? His ability to love is so much bigger than ours!

When I walk in humility, I embrace grace. I embrace God's love, and I welcome every part of Him so that He can be conformed into every part of me. Through humility, I can authentically come to the place where Paul says,

> *"It is not I who live anymore, but Christ who lives in me"*
> *(Galatians 2:20).*

When I walk in humility, I welcome everything God has done for me and will continue to do through me for all of eternity, without question. I yield to my new nature because God has planted the divine "yes and amen" inside of me. As I come into agreement with who I am in Christ, I will automatically mature into who God intends me to be because all of God grows out of humility. I fully agree with God's plans and purpose for my life, and I want His will to be my will, so I say,

> *"Let it be to me according to your word" (Luke 1:38).*

Psalm 139:16, says God made a blueprint of our lives before we were even on the earth. And Ephesians 2:4-7 tells us,

> *But God, who is rich in mercy, out of the great love with which he loved us, even when we were dead through our trespasses, made us alive together with Christ (by grace you have been saved), and raised us up with him, and made us sit with him in the heavenly places in Christ Jesus, that in the coming ages he might show the immeasurable riches of his grace in kindness toward us in Christ Jesus.*

We are seated with Him in heavenly places in Christ Jesus, and when we allow Him to be everything in our life, we can abide in our seated position.

In his book, "Humility," Andrew Murray grasped its very heart, so I have included a few of his quotes in this chapter.

- *"Humility wakes up in you everything that belongs to God and imparts it into your life."*

- *"Humility is not so much a grace or virtue along with others; it is the root of all, because it alone takes the right attitude before God, and allows Him as God to be all."*

- *"Humility is death to self and life to the new nature of Christ. God resists the proud and gives grace to the humble. Grace, faith, and love grow out of the soil of humility, where there is selflessness. Self doesn't exist there."*

- *"Humility, the place of entire dependence on God, is the first duty and the highest virtue of the creature, and the root of every virtue. And so pride, or the loss of this humility, is the root of every sin and evil."*

- *"Humility is the only soil in which the graces root; the lack of humility is the sufficient explanation of every defect and failure.*

- *"Spiritual growth develops out of the soil of humility."*

- *"Humility boosts us up to the highest purpose of God, to conform us to His Son."*

- *"Pride must die in us, or nothing of heaven can live in us."*

- *"Humility is nothing but the disappearance of self in the vision that God is all."*

- *"The Holy Spirit is free to lead us and guide us into all truth through humility."*

- *"The Lamb of God has placed within us His Spirit of a meek and lowly heart, full of love to serve others. Indeed, to be the servant of all is the Spirit of Humility."*

- *"Humility wakes up in us what belongs to God, and what belongs to God changes us and conforms us and transforms us into the image of Christ."*

- *"Self has no voice in humility, where only the voice of our Shepherd is entertained."*

- *"Humility is perfect quietness of heart. It is to expect nothing, to wonder at nothing that is done to me, to feel nothing done against me. It is to be at rest when nobody praises me, and when I am blamed or despised. It is to have a blessed home in the Lord, where I can go in and shut the door, and kneel to my Father in secret, and am at peace as in a deep sea of calmness, when all around and above is trouble."*

CHAPTER FIVE

IT TAKES HUMILITY TO RUN TO HIM

HUMILITY HAS NOTHING TO DO with condemnation and has everything to do with being jam-packed full of God and the *real* kingdom we live in. I must allow the Humble Lamb of God who dwells on the inside of my spirit, to possess my mind, my heart, my soul, and my body. I can only abide in real freedom when I allow Him to inhabit all of me.

> *Come to me, all who labor and are heavy laden, and I will give you rest. Take my yoke upon you, and learn from me; for I am gentle and lowly in heart, and you will find rest for your souls. For my yoke is easy, and my burden is light"* (Matthew 11:28).

"Come unto me."

Those are the three greatest words you will ever hear out of the mouth of your Savior.

"Come to me in your time of need."

"Seek me out in your time of rebellion."

"Pursue me in your time of sin."

"Call to me in your time of sickness."

"Look for me in your time of worry."

"Search for me in your time of repentance."

"Just come unto me."

Jesus has not changed those three words, ever. He will always say, *"Come to me,"* and we will be welcome to run into His arms. I will always yearn to hear Him say, *"Come to me,"* and I will always want to live in His presence. However, I will only go to Him when I'm humble.

Let's say you got up this morning and you did something you know wasn't right. Just get away with the Lord. Go to Him quickly, and He'll fix it. You can take the old man right out of your life because he has been crucified, and replace him with the Lamb of God, and with His life. When I am humble, I can run into His arms and let Him repair whatever I have done wrong. Self, however, cannot do this and will instead be ruled by condemnation.

Whenever my father called me using my middle name it got

my attention because I knew it was serious. And whenever I used my own children's middle names, it got their attention, too. They knew I meant business. I've seen Christians who know they've done something dumb, and they think they can fix it by works. They decide to pray more or read the Word more. They're trying, in their own strength, to do something only God can do in their lives. I have been guilty of this, myself.

One day I heard the Father say,

"Richard Carroll..." and I knew He meant business.

"Yes, Sir?"

"Are you telling me you think you can do something greater than the sacrifice of my Son? Are you telling me your self-righteous works are greater than the tormenting of..."

Then I had a vision of His horrible, painful death and I fell on my face, weeping; and then I begged God not to kill me because of my self-righteous attitude. I had assumed I could do something good enough that God would have to consider my works above His Son's sacrifice. I can honestly say this destroyed self-righteousness in me forever. Then the Lord added,

"Unless you treat your old man as an enemy he'll rule your life."

When the Father calls you by your middle name, you're going to listen, but it set me free. Now, when I do something stupid, I go to Him quickly because I know there is absolutely nothing I could ever do that would be good enough to fix whatever I just did wrong. I don't have the liberty of saying, "Oh well, I'll go to church more. I'll pray more. I'll do this more..." This is self-righteousness, and it completely denies God's ultimate sacrifice.

Jesus has promised us rest. When we were born again, we were born of His Spirit. That Spirit is in us, and whenever I go to Him, He gives rest to my soul. He hears me. He strengthens me. He gives me value, cleanses me from all unrighteousness and applies His own blood to my transgressions before the throne of grace. Jesus is for me and continuously intercedes on my behalf.

God loved us so much that He sacrificed His own Son. Jesus loved us so much, He gave Himself for the Father, and the Holy Spirit has come to ensure everything Jesus and the Father completed becomes fulfilled in our lives. We only need to accept His grace and forgiveness.

I love being overwhelmed by the Lamb, but self doesn't. Self, the fallen man in fallen nature, only lives for Himself. He lives for no other purpose. He can be giving and kind, and he can care for people, love people, and help people; but the fallen nature is ultimately self-motivated. That's why Paul said, "In my old self, there is nothing good" (Romans 7:18). When you humble yourself, everything that is not of God will dissolve from your life, and everything which is of God will fill its place.

Let's look at the Lamb of God in the book of Revelation. I don't try to figure it out; I just read it, and the Bible says I'll get blessed. Kenneth Hagin said three of his Antichrists died, so he quit trying to tell everybody who the Antichrist was. That's just one of those stupid controversies. I don't care who Antichrist is because it says the bright shining of the King of kings will destroy him! Hallelujah! That's what I choose to focus on. That bright shining One lives inside of us. Greater is He that is in us, than the defeated foe who's coming into the world. Jesus is our king!

> *Then I looked, and I heard around the throne and the*
> *living creatures and the elders the voice of many angels,*
> *numbering myriads of myriads and thousands of*
> *thousands, saying with a loud voice, "Worthy is the*
> *Lamb who was slain, to receive power and wealth and*
> *wisdom and might and honor and glory and*
> *blessing!" And I heard every creature in heaven and on*
> *earth and under the earth and in the sea, and all therein,*
> *saying, "To him who sits upon the throne and to the*
> *Lamb be blessing and honor and glory and might for*
> *ever and ever!" (Revelation 5:11).*

Look who is being glorified in heaven! It's the Lamb who was slain, the eternal Humble One. The reason the Lamb of God is worthy to receive glory and power is that He humbled Himself. If He had not humbled Himself, we wouldn't have salvation. He didn't redeem us by using His power; it was through His humility. He was raised in power, but His humility saved us, and His humility keeps us alive. Remember, He is always interceding on our behalf. Jesus is meek and lowly, and we can only enter His fullness through humility. As we humble ourselves and yield to the Lord, He gives us enough grace to allow humility to permeate our life. Humility is our highest blessing, and it unlocks all the kingdom of heaven to us.

Pride is our greatest enemy because it prohibits God from maneuvering in our life. Why? Because we choose to walk in the world, where we are validated by works. "Look how great I am, Lord! Have I not saved these many people? Haven't I preached the gospel? Have I not done this, Lord? Have I not done that, Lord?"

Jesus will reply, *"I don't know who are, you workers of iniquity! It's lawlessness. You're working in your own strength, and you're trying to prove yourself to man and me."*

Paul said,

> *You yourselves are our letter of recommendation, written*
> *on your hearts, to be known and read by all men*
> *(2 Corinthians 3:2).*

We are living epistles of the Lord Jesus Christ. I am like Jesus in many areas of my life, and I recognize other areas that still need to change. If I couldn't say this, I would be walking in false humility. You may think, "Oh, I could never say that." Well then, you're full of pride. Freely acknowledge that you are co-laboring with Christ to be transformed by grace, and let God fill you entirely with Himself.

You can't do this through condemnation, and you can't do it by any effort of self, so don't beat yourself up and think, "Well, I *should* be doing this..." because works will get you nowhere. Instead, say, "Thank you, Jesus. You've already done it for me! Go ahead, Holy Spirit! Take the humility of the Lamb and put it in those areas where you know I need it. I know you're not mad at me, even though I really blew it. Thank you, Lord." God wants His kingdom in your life so that you will recognize it in yourself, and others will see it in you.

With great humility comes great power because it's no longer the old man who lives; it's Christ living in us. Christ lives in us and prays for us as we become more and more like Him. When you make a mistake, humility will compel you to run into His arms quickly so that He can fix it. Otherwise, you can open the door to condemnation, which creates a distance between you and the One who loves you more than you could ever fathom. Works are futile in this situation. Jesus will always be waiting for you to go to Him so that He can give you peace about whatever is bothering you. You don't have to be perfect, but you must have a heart that is willing to be perfected.

CHAPTER SIX

I DID NOT RECEIVE THIS
GRACE IN VAIN

IT TAKES THE GRACE OF GOD to live a Christian life. We have been forgiven according to the riches of God's grace, and grace drives our transformation from the old to the new creation in Christ. God's grace also propels our spiritual growth, which doesn't happen overnight. We

> *"...grow in the grace and knowledge of our Lord and Savior Jesus Christ" (2 Peter 3:18).*

Grace transforms our thinking, ambitions, motivations, and behavior. In fact, God's gift of grace empowers everything we do in our daily Christian life. In 1st Corinthians 15, Paul said,

For I am the least of the apostles, unfit to be called an apostle, because I persecuted the church of God. But by the grace of God I am what I am, and his grace toward me was not in vain. On the contrary, I worked harder than any of them, though it was not I, but the grace of God which is with me.

Let's take a closer look at this passage to see what Paul is saying.

"For I am the least of the apostles, unfit to be called an apostle, because I persecuted the church of God."

Paul is not expressing a shameful self-image; it's a redeemed one! Although Paul was not proud of the things he did before he met Jesus, he fully embraced God's grace and forgiveness and recognized that he was a brand-new creation. Grace enabled him to move beyond his past, and he did not allow guilt to weigh him down or hinder him from doing everything God called him to do. Although Paul never forgot where he came from, he understood that Saul, the old man, was the guilty one; and he died the very moment he accepted Christ as his Savior. Paul is saying, "That's who I *was*, but it's not who I *am*, anymore!"

If you ever forget where you came from, you'll find yourself judging other people. I used to be a drunk. I fought, ran around, and did all kinds of crazy things the world does until I finally decided my life was not worth living. That's who I was, but it's not who I am anymore. However, I never forget where I came from, and I know the only One who brought me out of it was Jesus.

If you're doing the things I used to do I won't condemn you out of self-righteousness. I started smoking when I was twelve years old, but God delivered me from cigarettes. Although I don't smoke anymore, I can still sit around people who do; and it doesn't bother me because I know I used to smell just like them. Unfortunately, I have seen many Christians who have also been delivered from smoking who have no problem saying, *"Boy, you sure do stink!"* They completely forget that they used to smell the same way! Smokers don't bother me because I know I can bring the freedom of Christ to them. If I sit by someone who gets drunk in front of me, I have no room to condemn them because I used to be just like them, and I know God can set them free.

How about you? You might have been an old drunk or a drug addict at one time. If you ever forget where you came from, you will never be able to help others in the same situation that God delivered you from. We should be saying, "I know where you're at, and I know the One who can deliver you! I've come to bring His love to you, and not condemnation." An attitude of self-righteous condemnation will ensure that person will stay in bondage, but grace always brings liberty and finds a way to set people free.

Instead of condemning a person, speak that which imparts grace to the ears of the hearer. Speak that which imparts God. Speak that which gives hope. Speak that which encourages. Speak that which conveys healing. Speak that which reveals the love of God to somebody else, instead of your judgment. The love of God doesn't sneak around people's backs saying one thing to them and then saying something different about them to other people.

Let me share some good news with you. If you're dealing with some of these issues, all you need to do is humble yourself and say, "God, I need grace in this area." Don't beat yourself up because you can't do it in your strength. That's the benefit of grace!

I couldn't stop drinking, smoking, fighting and hating on my own. I couldn't overcome unforgiveness. I could not overcome any of those things in my own strength; but when I let Jesus take control of my life, they all went away. When we are dealing with issues, the Holy Spirit says, "Look, here's a sin which is a problem in your life. Give it to me and let grace work on it."

"But by the grace of God I am what I am..."

We are who we are by the grace of God. We can say this because we are not capable of doing this in our own strength; it's grace working in and through us which enables us to overcome the sins and issues in our lives.

"...and his grace toward me was not in vain."

Paul is asserting that he didn't receive the grace of God and then bury it on the inside. In other words, he did not squander or waste it but gratefully accepted it. Although this gift of grace was purchased at an extraordinarily high price, we can choose to deny it. We can say no to what God wants to do in our lives, resist change, and do our own thing. If we grieve the Holy Spirit through selfishness, this will stop grace from transforming us into what God has called us to be and will hinder what God can fully do in our lives.

We are the body of Christ, and God asks us to co-labor with Him. This means we cooperate with the Spirit of Grace and allow Him to make changes in our lives. We were created in Christ Jesus for good works, and we are His artistry and workmanship. Christ is the head, we are His body, and we release His power on earth.

God lovingly placed so much inside of us when we were born again. Grace compels us to realize that He needs us to carry out His plans and purposes on earth and equips us to do everything

He called us to do before the foundation of the world. God put such a treasure in our earthen vessel, and by our faith and obedience, we become stewards of His grace. Let it transform you into who you are intended to be, and you will understand that it isn't self, but the Spirit of Grace working through you.

"On the contrary, I worked harder than any of them..."

It would be easy to say, "Wow, Paul, it sounds like you are awfully full of pride. You're telling everybody you work harder than I do!"

But Paul could respond, "Yeah, but it's not me; it's God's grace!" Paul knew he lived by grace, and he was actually saying, "Grace enables me to do everything I do. My whole life is grace working through me, and that's why I have worked harder than the others. It wasn't me; it was only by grace."

The only way he could have survived being beaten five times was grace. The only way he could have been stoned and raised from the dead was grace. The only way he could have lived through floating at sea for three days was grace. The only way he could have endured the prisons in those days was grace. The power of God's grace was manifested in him; healing his body and keeping it strong and healthy. No physical body could have survived what Paul endured unless it was full of grace. He was only able to do everything he did because of the power working within him.

Paul attributed everything in his life and everything he accomplished to the grace of God. God's grace is also working in us. It's a power and a force, molding us into the very image of Christ. I'm getting stronger in grace every day. Actually, grace is getting stronger in me! The more I exalt grace in my life, the less the old man has to say. Everything good in me was placed there by God Himself, so I am only good by virtue of God. The old man has nothing to do with it, except to mess it up, because there is nothing good in my flesh. Don't inhibit its work in your life because of self, doubt, or unbelief. Instead, yield and allow grace to work, and do everything it can do.

CHAPTER SEVEN

HUMILITY EMBRACES GRACE

A TRANSFORMATION BEGAN the very moment you accepted Christ. Some of you may not be able to recognize much of Jesus in yourself, even if you received Him many years ago. You may be wondering, "Well, if the Holy Spirit and the Word of God are working in me, why am I not a whole lot more like Jesus by now?"

Many people never humble themselves enough to yield to the Spirit of Grace when He starts making adjustments in their lives. We cannot do anything for God or change anything within ourselves without the Spirit of Grace. Humility embraces grace. What does self do? Self only embraces self and the things of the world. John the Baptist said,

> *"Behold, the Lamb of God, who takes away the sin of the world" (John 1:29).*

Notice he didn't say "sins" plural, but instead said, "sin." Sinners are not sinners because they sin; they sin because they're sinners. They have a fallen nature and don't possess the new nature. We were all inclined to follow the lust of the flesh, the lust of the eyes and the pride of life before we became born again because we did not have the Spirit of Grace working in us.

The Holy Spirit was poured out on the day of Pentecost so that all could come to the Lord Jesus Christ through the preaching of the gospel. This wasn't possible under the old covenant because the Holy Spirit only rested upon kings, priests, and judges. But now, under the New Covenant, the Holy Spirit is available to everyone. This doesn't mean everyone has the Spirit of God in them, but when we receive Christ, the Spirit of Grace comes in, and we're born again. The first step in humbling ourselves is recognizing we need a Savior and there is absolutely nothing we can do to save ourselves. The Holy Spirit came with a two-fold mission of grace. The first thing He did was kill the old man. He crucified him by putting him on the cross with Christ, and then He raised up a brand-new man on the inside of us, which is a brand-new creation.

Our spirit became one with Christ, but what is in our spirit must then develop and flow into our soul, our thinking, our mind, and even into our body; which is the temple of the Holy Spirit. This temple no longer belongs to us and has become God's property. Humility allows us to do things God's way.

Becoming humble is a work of grace, but we must decide to embrace it. Believe it or not, the new man, the *real* you, is humble because you've been born of the Humble One. You have the humility of Christ in your spirit, but the next step is to allow this grace to mature. The new you, created in the image of Christ, will never embrace the world or the things of the flesh because our new man only embraces God. When we humble ourselves, God will exalt us and give us grace. On the other hand, the old man (self) cannot embrace God. In fact, he's hostile toward God, so he was crucified.

If you want to know whether you're living in grace ask,

"Where is God in my life compared to myself?"

It's an obvious benchmark. Self-gravitates to the world and naturally prefers things which are not of God, but the new man draws toward God. He has given us sufficient grace to do this. Now we can live as a new creation which is always full of humility and embraces all of God's grace. Our new man enthusiastically receives *all* things of God, as well as His entire Word.

We live by grace through faith, and grace is a conforming and transforming work of God. Let me put it this way; grace is our life because Christ is our life. God is our life, so grace works. Grace conforms us to the image of Christ, and grace will never condone sin; in fact, it destroys sin. Sin no longer has dominion over us.

The Greek word for sin is "hamartia," which means "to miss the mark." If you've ever thrown darts or shot arrows, you know the goal is to hit the bullseye. Since the word "sin" means to miss the mark, whenever you sin, you have missed the bullseye. Big sins are easy to recognize like adultery, murder, or stealing; but what about sowing discord among the brethren? That's about as great a sin as anything else. How about worry or unbelief? Sin is merely missing the mark of what grace has been established in our life to accomplish.

Jesus was born for this very purpose. He destroyed the works of the devil, so sin is not our problem. Surprisingly, the devil is not our problem, either. Our problem is self. Self resists humility which allows the grace of God to alter the way we think and how we act. Self even impedes healing from flowing into our bodies.

Grace has been getting a bad rap lately because so-called grace teachers have been propagandizing that you can do anything you want "...because you're under grace now." They are mistaken, and this is false teaching. Paul said he was free to do anything he wanted, but he would not do anything unbeneficial to God. Paul understood his freedom but added,

> *"For you were called to freedom, brethren; only do not use your freedom as an opportunity for the flesh, but through love be servants of one another" (Galatians 5:13).*

Grace is not some substance floating around out there; it is God Himself directly imparted to you. Grace is God working in you, conforming your spirit, soul, and body into His image and likeness; therefore, grace does not tolerate sin. We sin when we judge other people, or when we try to "straighten out" the body of Christ. We have no business doing those things. We just need to let God straighten *us* out.

On the other hand, when you know that Jesus is the answer, and you are working as His representative, that is grace. Grace allows you to represent Jesus in every area of your life and will not sanction any part of your flesh working in you. Grace doesn't like your flesh; He destroyed it. He loves your spirit because you're born again of the Spirit of God, but we must submit ourselves to Him and love Him more than anything or anyone else. We must also love Him even more than ourselves. Grace is God. It's His attribute and His very essence. I'm going to make a bold statement here, and I won't apologize for it: If I live in humility, I *cannot* sin.

As a Christian, I can choose to sow to the flesh or sow to the spirit. It would be nice if the Lord hadn't given us a choice, but He did. My greatest fear is that when I stand before the Lord, I would be found to have done everything in my own strength and missed out on the fullness of His grace; which means I would have fallen far short of what He could have accomplished in my life. We should love God so much that self would choose to withdraw. The Bible says to

"...work out your own salvation with fear and trembling" *(Philippians 2:12).*

I fear and tremble whenever I think about doing anything *not* of God, and I can only do this by grace because it's impossible in my own strength. I've tried, and it doesn't work. I've even tried to crucify myself, and I couldn't do that, either. But Galatians 2:20 says I am crucified with Christ, so the old man is dead, and I'm alive in Christ Jesus.

Grace is God's power and ability to conform us to His image and likeness. This will help us to avoid sin and ensure that our thoughts begin to agree with His. Grace thinks about things which are lovely and true. It imparts to us the very mind of Christ and turns our body into a vessel of the Holy Spirit, alive with healing and good health. Grace changes our heart, and it's out of our heart that we believe.

Every day I get up and thank God for His grace. I go to bed and thank God for His grace. I wake up and say, "Thank you!" because I am one with Him and grace is my life, permeating me with more of Christ every day. Do I ever feel bad or get depressed? I don't know; I don't pay much attention to those things because I am just not interested in myself anymore, or in what my old self wants. Am I there yet? Not yet, but I'm on my way! I have the great privilege of allowing the grace of God to work in my life. When we do our part, God is always faithful to do the rest.

In Philippians 3:17, Paul said that if he was following the

Lord, to follow him. He also said to,

"... lay aside every weight, and sin which clings so closely, and let us run with perseverance the race that is set before us, looking to Jesus the pioneer and perfecter of our faith" (Hebrews 12:2).

Let God's Word be your life. Let it be your world. Let it be your identity! Then righteousness, peace, and joy will emerge in your life. Grace fills me with joy, happiness, and heaven! Grace fills me with God! It conforms me to the image of Christ. These days I'm happy and joyful, but in the past, I was a lot like Eeyore. You know, the old gray donkey in the classic A.A. Milne children series, *Winnie the Pooh*. Eeyore was always depressed, pessimistic, and down cast. But then I decided to become a Tigger and bounce around and be happy instead! I could not have done any of this in my own strength. It was grace which enabled me to stop paying attention to myself.

I never want to do anything to disgrace God, snub the Spirit of Grace or disparage the Blood of Jesus. I don't have the liberty to sin, and neither do you. I do, however, have the freedom to love and to be full of the Holy Spirit and live the way God wants me to live. That's real freedom, and Christ set me free. Why in the world would you love anyone or anything more than God?

If someone cuts you off in traffic, or if you're in Walmart, and the person in front of you takes 15 minutes to check out, those are small things, but they can turn into big ones if you allow them to frustrate you. If anything frustrates you, it's not God. You may tell yourself through gritted teeth, "I have patience. I'm full of patience. I'm not mad. I'm not mad at that person...."

If you're using self to correct yourself, you're not letting patience work in you. Remember, you can do all things through Christ who strengthens you. Don't try to do it in your own strength when grace makes it so much easier. When the Spirit of

Grace is working in you, you're not mad, and you're not frustrated. Grace gives you the ability to stand calmly and patiently in line and not be upset. If you happen to notice how exasperated the clerk is, grace will provide you with the ability to smile at her. I guarantee the love of Christ will move through you when you smile and say, "It's okay. Don't worry about it." You just released grace and love to that person because you are abiding in it. You can't make it happen on your own, and you can't do it without grace.

Whenever someone runs me off the road, I recall a few times I have done the same thing to somebody else, instead of wanting to chase them down. This is evidence of God's grace working in me. It's also working in you. One day something happens, and you suddenly realize, "Hey! I'm not responding the way I used to!" Why? Because that old person is dead.

When my son was about three years old, I would say, "You turkey!" whenever someone aggravated me in traffic. One Thanksgiving as we were cooking, I told him, "This is a turkey." He said, "*That's* a turkey???! I thought turkeys were those people out there you talk to all the time." This is a true story, and God used a child to correct me.

That "turkey anointing" still springs up occasionally, but the grace of God is so much greater. Why should I allow some stranger to ruin my day? It would be easy to go to work and say, "Man, I got cut off in traffic this morning," and spend the whole day complaining about whoever cut you off on the freeway. Do you realize that you are giving a stranger control over your life? Instead, let Jesus control your life.

When you humble yourself and embrace grace, Jesus does the work you can't do. Grace conforms you to His image. He makes it real. Grace will cause us to make room for God to work His perfect plan and purpose in and through us, as well as His desires, His power, and His kingdom.

We are stewards of the manifold grace of God, and He gives more grace to those who humble themselves. Grace will take you to the ends of the earth and will also move you into things that will make your flesh uncomfortable. When grace starts working in your life, you will start becoming the person God called you to be.

We have no good works of our own, but God has given us stewardship of the works of grace He has assigned to us. We should not allow feelings, people, or other things of the flesh to prevent us from allowing grace to transform us into the image of Christ.

The most obvious sin in the body of Christ is people doing their own thing instead of yielding to the very One who gave His life so that He could live through us. Our lives are no longer our own. As we surrender to Him, He will take us to places and do things in our lives beyond our imagination.

Self focuses on self. "I don't have any money." "My marriage is a wreck." "People don't like me." That kind of thinking is focusing on self, but grace won't allow me to think that way anymore. I used to, but not anymore! Allow grace to do its work in you, and you will eventually realize there isn't much of the old you left.

My ability to preach may be a great thing, but it's not about me at all. I can only do what the grace of God enables me to do. It's all about Him now, and not me because it's not my life; it's His. Whenever I obey grace, I discover God has filled me with even more of Himself.

Are you full of grace today? Answer these questions, and it may give you some idea of where grace is, compared to self.

How much of your old self is not there anymore?

How much time do you spend thinking about yourself?

How much time do you spend telling others about yourself?

How often do you find yourself dominating conversations by talking about yourself?

How often can you sit with the body of Christ, and only speak as the Holy Spirit would prompt you to talk?

You may *think* you have the right to speak your mind, but the Word says that you are only entitled to speak to (and about) others with grace and blessing. If you say things that would hurt someone or damage their reputation, you aren't operating in grace. The adage is true; "If you can't say something nice, then don't say anything at all." God is love and grace, and we are to follow His example.

CHAPTER EIGHT

THE SEEDS OF GRACE

A S PAUL WAS LEAVING EPHESUS, he said,

> *"And now I commend you to God and to the Word of His grace, which is able to build you up and to give you the inheritance among all those who are sanctified" (Acts 20:32).*

To *commend* means to entrust or to commit to the care of another. Paul could rest assured the Word would encourage and sanctify them. Jesus said,

> *"Sanctify them in the truth; thy word is truth" (John 17:17).*

The Word of God sanctifies us and sets us apart. *Sanctified* means to be made holy. You are already holy, and you are endlessly being transformed into God's image and likeness as the Word works in us. The Holy Spirit is central to this process because, without Him, the Word of God becomes the law.

"To be a minister of Christ Jesus to the Gentiles in the priestly service of the gospel of God, so that the offering of the Gentiles may be acceptable, sanctified by the Holy Spirit" (Romans 15:16).

The Holy Spirit will only sanctify the Word of God, which is Truth. He will not bless our opinions, our doctrines or our traditions. He also sanctifies God's people. So, we are sanctified and set apart for God by the Holy Spirit and the Word of God. If we try to comprehend this Word with our natural understanding, we will be unable to grasp it.

I have heard people ask, "Are you in the Word?" We need to turn this question around and ask, "Is the Word in *you*? Is the Word *working* in you?" God wants His Word working in you because you were born again of His incorruptible seed. It is already on the inside of you, and it will accomplish whatever it sets out to do, working by the power of the Holy Spirit.

The Word of God is a seed. Here is the parable of the sower.

The sower sows the word. And these are the ones along the path, where the word is sown: when they hear, Satan immediately comes and takes away the word that is sown in them. And these are the ones sown on rocky ground: the ones who, when they hear the word, immediately receive it with joy. And they have no root in themselves, but endure for a while; then, when tribulation or persecution arises on account of the word, immediately they fall away. And others are the ones sown among thorns. They are those who hear the word, but the cares of the world and the deceitfulness of riches and the desires for other things enter in and choke the word, and it proves unfruitful. But those that were sown on the good soil are the ones who hear the word and accept it and bear fruit, thirtyfold and sixtyfold and a hundredfold (Mark 14:4-20).

We all experience various soils at different times in our lives, and you can expect many opportunities in your life for good seeds to be yanked out of your heart and exchanged for bad ones.

I'm a farmer. I was raised in a farming community. Seeds germinate in soil, and farmers know about seedtime and harvest. You plant wheat in September, and you plant milo and corn in the spring because each one has a specific growing period. Farmers also know the soil determines the growth of the plant. Farmers cultivate the land by working it and fertilizing it to prepare it for planting. They know the better the soil, the better their harvest will be, and soil is no respecter of seed. If you plant good seed in it, the seed will thrive. And if you plant weeds in the ground, the earth will nourish them, and they will flourish. The soil automatically cultivates whatever seeds we sow.

Jesus said our heart is the soil where the Word of God is planted. Just as the soil is no respecter of seed, your heart will automatically produce whatever seeds you have sown into your thinking, into your body, and even into your lifestyle. If you plant seeds of doubt, unbelief, anger, bitterness, and unforgiveness, your heart will germinate those things and produce them in your life. Whatever you sow there is what will grow there.

If you want to know what's growing in your heart, listen to what is coming out of your mouth. What are you saying? You cultivate seeds by what you believe in your heart and speak with your mouth. Faith works the same way. Jesus put it this way;

you will talk about whatever is in abundance in your heart. If you have an abundance of the world in your heart, you'll mostly talk about worldly things. Some Word may occasionally show up in your conversation, but the majority of what you'll find yourself discussing will be of the world.

I quit planting gardens because I just ended up having to mow the weeds. Those weeds outgrew whatever I had planted because I hadn't cultivated the soil properly, and I didn't take care of it well. Sometimes I could move the weeds aside and find a little cucumber or something down there, but it wasn't very productive because weeds had overtaken it. I can sow some Word in my heart, but if I'm planting more of the world in there, the world will choke out the Word, just like those weeds in my garden. My point is, the Word of God works out of the meditation of our heart. Here's what it will do in your life:

> *...and how from childhood you have been acquainted with the sacred writings which are able to instruct you for salvation through faith in Christ Jesus. All scripture is inspired by God and profitable for teaching, for reproof, for correction, and for training in righteousness, that the man of God may be complete, equipped for every good work (2 Timothy 3:15-17).*

God's Word works like any other seed. The Holy Spirit takes what we have planted, waters it, and it produces righteousness and salvation in you. It encourages, sanctifies, corrects and directs you. It will renew your mind so that you can become like Christ. It trains you in righteousness and equips you to do every work for God. The Word does the work, so we don't have to. Our job is to yield to the working of the Holy Spirit and the Word of God and allow them to replace bad seeds with good ones. If you plant an acorn, it will become an oak tree. If it's an apple seed, it will produce an apple tree. If you have planted a weed, it's only going to become a bigger weed.

Farmers know various seeds must be sown at different depths. If you don't correctly plant the seed in the soil, it won't produce. Some seeds should be sown down deep, and others are scattered closer to the surface. The height and the strength of the plant are determined by its root system. The deeper the root system, the bigger it will become.

One of the heartiest grains you can grow is wheat. You plant it in September, and two or three months later the field becomes stooled over with beautiful green plants. Cattle can even feed on it. Then winter comes, and the lush green field turns yellow. To the natural eye, it appears that the wheat has died. That's deceptive, because wheat roots down during the winter months, and in the spring, little sprouts of grain begin to appear. Then it grows until June when it's time to harvest.

And so, it is in our lives. There are seedtime and harvest, and just when it looks like the Word is barren in your life, the depth of its root system will determine its strength. We want to pop the seed in and instantly see growth take place, but you can't plant an acorn one day and then say, "Look! Now I'm a big oak tree!" the next day. It doesn't work that way. Just as seeds need time to grow, it also takes time for the Holy Spirit to develop the Word of God in us.

> *"Therefore put away all filthiness and rank growth of wickedness..."(James 1:21).*

If we want the Word to grow in our hearts and mature in our lives, we must stop planting seeds of filthiness and wickedness. What you see, hear, and meditate on determines which seeds you are planting in your heart. The Scripture says Lot vexed his righteous soul by the things he saw and heard. We live in a world full of wickedness and filthiness, and most people spend more time on social media, their cell phone, and their favorite TV programs than in the Word of God. This means most people are planting way more seeds of the world than of the Word, and we are reaping what we have sown.

The Holy Spirit is after something in you. In fact, He wants *you*. Every bit of you! He wants you to be entirely His. He wants you to be completely free, totally happy, utterly joyful, absolutely full of power, and unreservedly full of love. He wants all the weeds of the flesh pulled out, and He wants to replace them with the Word of God. When the Word is working in you, you won't be fearful; you'll be faithful.

We must receive the Word of God with meekness, and meekness is another word for humility. Meekness means I will choose to put the Word of God first -- before my opinion, above my feelings, over my own life, and beyond what I want. I will take self out of the picture, and as I receive the Word of God with meekness, I will obey it.

> *"...and receive with meekness the implanted word, which is able to save your souls" (James 1:21).*

Notice this verse doesn't say *spirits*, it says *souls*. Do you know a lot of Christians will end up in heaven with their soul unsaved? They did their own thing and never submitted themselves to the Word of God in humility, so their soul was never renewed.

> *"Having purified your souls by your obedience to the truth for sincere love of the brethren, love one another earnestly from the heart" (1 Peter 1:22).*

If you want to know how much of God's Word is thriving in

your soul, examine how much you love your brothers and sisters. If you're judging and condemning others, you've obviously not planted the Word of God there. Instead, you've planted judgment, hatred, and jealousy, and it comes out by what you say about others. We can never forget that Jesus shed His blood for everybody. Jesus said,

> "...as you did it to one of the least of these my brethren, you did it to me" (Matthew 25:40).

Jesus takes it personally when you blast the body of Christ. He takes it personally when you judge or condemn somebody else. It's one thing to *hear* the Word of God, but it's another thing to *obey* it. Faith is believing and being obedient. The Word of God conforms us to the image of Christ but understand that you must receive it with obedience. Obedience is what humility is all about. Dear brothers and sisters, there is no excuse. God has said, *"I've given you my Word of Grace. I want to build you up. I want you to be conformed to my image and likeness."*

You can always get the Word of God in you if you have the desire, no matter what your circumstances are. If you can see, you can read it. If you can hear, you can listen to it. There are many ways God can get His Word into your heart, but it's up to you to open your heart to receive it. This is our identity. What we put into our heart is so important because it will produce whatever we have sown. Read this again:

> "Having purified your souls by your obedience to the truth for sincere love of the brethren, love one another earnestly from the heart" "You have been born anew, not of perishable seed but of imperishable, through the living and abiding word of God" (1 Peter 1:22,23).

The evidence of a purified soul is how much you love others. Jesus is the Living Word of God and the Spirit of Life. The Holy Spirit uses His words to produce life in your mind and body, and this creates a transformation in you. You've been born again by this incorruptible seed, the Word of God, for all flesh is like grass; all the glory of the flowers, like grass.

> *"The grass withers, the flower fades; but the word of our God will stand forever" (Isaiah 40:8).*

Whatever you plant in your heart outside of the Word of God will perish. All your worries, your doubts, your confusion, your judgments, and your frustrations will disappear. Your social media accounts, your favorite movies, and your favorite sports teams will also cease to exist. Only the Word of God abides forever. I don't want any of us to stand before the Lord and hear Him say,

> *"Well, let's see... Let's pull all these weeds out. I only see about ten percent of my Word in you, but by the time I burn up all the wood, hay, and stubble in there, I'm afraid there just won't be much left to bless you with."*

You will still get to go to heaven, even though your rewards burned up, but only the Word of God in our heart abides forever. It is eternal and will never perish. It will abide in you forever because an infinite transformation has taken place in your life.

What a great privilege to receive the Word of God! His Word is the good news which is preached to you, and the Word doeth good like a medicine *(Proverbs 17:22)*. It will heal your bones and your heart. It will fill you with peace, joy, righteousness, and the kingdom of God. It will supply you with faith, fill you with abundance, and it will provide you with the blessings of heaven. Why wouldn't everyone want to plant God's Word in their heart?

If we plant more of the world in our heart, our heart will become hardened against the Word of God. If we continually plant fear in our lives, we have hardened our heart against the seed of faith. If we sow doubt, we will always be doubtful.

"Well, you know, if it weren't for bad luck I would have no luck at all." I will tell you right now that if you plant that kind of thinking, your heart will harden to the Word of God in those areas and you will be more open to depression, discouragement, lies, and anger. It's all about self, and whatever self you plant in your heart will perish, but the Word of God is incorruptible. It's forever. It transforms you *now* into the excellent condition you're going to abide in forever. I would rather plant the Word in my heart than anything else in this life. That's why I spend a lot of time in the Word. You need to fall in love with it. I need to have it every day because I love it, and revelation comes every time I read and meditate on it.

> *"So put away all malice and all guile and insincerity and envy and all slander" (1 Peter 2:1).*

In other words, stop sowing garbage in your heart. Yank those weeds out by the roots! Remember, whatever you plant in your heart will grow, and your heart is no respecter of the seeds you put in it. If you spend more time meditating on your job, sports, or your favorite teams or movies, the seeds of the world will choke out the Word of God.

> *"Like newborn babes, long for the pure spiritual milk, that by it you may grow up to salvation, for you have tasted the kindness of the Lord" (1 Peter 2:2,3).*

Every plant starts out as a tiny seed, and then it becomes a little shoot, and then it gets taller, and eventually, it will become a mature plant. In other words, it grows. There is a growth process in all of nature. You can't just put a little bit of Scripture in your heart and expect to suddenly become like Jesus. It doesn't work that way. The Word needs time to germinate and grow in our heart to choke out the old seeds and replace them with the kingdom of God. Before you know it, you're thinking and the way you say things will begin to change.

If you plant a garden, you won't need to tell me what you've sown. I'll just wait for it to grow and then I can tell you what you planted. If you plant squash, I'll say, "Hey, I see you planted squash!" when it starts to grow. Now, you could lie to me and tell me you planted watermelons, but when I come back to get a beautiful ripe watermelon, and there's nothing there but a bunch of squash (and I don't like squash) I'll know you lied to me. You told me you planted watermelon, and I was expecting watermelon, not squash. You can lie to me, but you can't lie to God.

"Thus you will know them by their fruits" (Matthew 7:20.)

What comes out of your mouth when it's harvest time? What is in you when you hit a brick wall? When you face adversity, whatever you have planted in your heart will be apparent, and if it wasn't the Word of God it's not going to be watermelon; it's going to be squash.

CHAPTER NINE

THE PERSONAL EVIDENCE OF GRACE

WHEN GRACE MANIFESTS YOU CAN SEE IT, you can hear it, you can feel it, and you will fully experience it. It is the same today as it was in the book of Acts, and no matter what others may say, God is the still the same today as He was back then.

> *"And the multitudes with one accord gave heed to what was said by Philip, when they heard him and saw the signs which he did" (Acts 8:6).*

> *"Even Simon Himself believed, and after being baptized he continued with Philip. And seeing signs and great miracles performed, he was amazed" (Acts 8:13).*

The word *amazed* means it blew his mind and was beyond

anything he could have ever imagined.

"...and the hand of the Lord was with them" (Acts 11: 21).

The hand of the Lord means *God's presence.* The Amplified says,

"...the presence of the Lord was with them in power."

Whenever we see a reference to the Lord stretching out His hand, it signifies the presence of God, the glory of God, and the majesty of God manifested in power.

" News of this came to the ears of the church in Jerusalem, and they sent Barnabas to Antioch. When he came and saw the grace of God, he was glad; and exhorted them..." (Acts 11:22-23).

Barnabus witnessed miracles, signs and wonders, and gifts of the Spirit in operation. They just naturally accompany the gospel. He saw God's grace in action as demons were cast out and people walked away healed. As a prophet, he confirmed these things and strengthened the church in Antioch.

"So they remained for a long time, speaking boldly for the Lord, who bore witness to the word of his grace, granting signs and wonders to be done by their hands" (Acts 14:3).

This is evidence of God's miraculous power with us.

How shall we escape if we neglect such a great salvation? It was declared at first by the Lord, and it was attested to us by those who heard him, while God also bore witness by

signs and wonders and various miracles and by gifts of the Holy Spirit distributed according to his own will (Hebrews 2:3-4).

Operating in the gifts of the Spirit is confirmation that the Holy Spirit and the Word are working through us. Paul said,

"My little children with whom I am again in travail until Christ be formed in you" (Galatians 4:19).

In other words, Paul is saying here, "I travail until people can see Christ fully developed in your lives and your nature."

I understand this verse because my entire heart's desire is to present every man and woman to God as mature Christians, and I often experience a deep travail to see Christ formed in you. Paul is warning us that we can permanently restrict the grace inside of us if we don't renew our minds and remain selfish, self-centered Christians.

If I took you to court and tried you for being a Christian, would there be enough evidence of God's grace working in your life to convict you? Can people look at you and see Christ? When grace is at work in you, it will bring fullness and abundance to your life. It doesn't take long to realize how shallow and empty the things of the world are once you have experienced the kingdom of God. God placed His kingdom in us, and we are called to walk in it. We are His instruments of righteousness.

You may think, "I'm not good." Well, you're believing a lie. Okay, your flesh isn't good, but it has been crucified, and it's dead. When you put on the new man and live in grace, the goodness of God is imparted to your mind, your heart, your soul, and your body, so you are the express goodness of God on this earth. You are the temple of the Holy Ghost. You are good by virtue of God, but you must choose to put goodness on, and you must decide to live in it.

Say, "I am good because of the grace of God." Now repeat it over and over until you believe it. I want everyone to be mature in Christ because there is greatness on the inside of us the world desperately needs.

> *"As each has received a gift, employ it for one another, as good stewards of God's varied grace" (1 Peter 4:10).*

It's astounding when you realize that Almighty God, who created the moon and stars, and everything else we can see, has also shined Himself into us. He is on the inside of us; however, we can refuse His grace and choose to disobey him.

God has given us stewardship; therefore, we are stewards of His grace, and we are His ambassadors. God gave man dominion over the works of His hands. Are you not a work of His hand? Therefore, you have authority over yourself; otherwise, you would obey God all the time and do everything He said to do. But considering your position, it becomes an act of your will to release the grace of God that's in you. You're the overseer and custodian of the grace He placed inside of you.

What is required of a steward? To be faithful. I refuse to allow tragedy, circumstances, what people think, whatever has happened in my life, or anything else to separate me from the love of God in Christ Jesus. Nothing will stop me from allowing His grace to work in and through me. Someday I will stand before Jesus, the only person who went to the cross for me. When I stand before Him, I will give an account of my stewardship, and I intend to be found faithful. Nobody else died for me, so I'm not concerned about what other people think. I want to obey my Master.

Remember the parables of the talents in Matthew 25? Each

man had to give an account of his stewardship of what he had been given. That was a parable about the church. We are stewards of everything God has given us. When you stand before Heaven, you won't be judged regarding your salvation because your name is in the Lamb's Book of Life, but there is another book there, and you will be held fully accountable for the stewardship of the grace which was granted to you. This is the reason we must humble ourselves. Humble, humble, humble, humble, grace, grace, grace, grace... until the old person disappears. We must do it until we live and impart grace in everything we say and do, and until Christ is revealed through us. We must do it until we are quick to repent and quick to change our heart and mind by the grace of God. We are all stewards of this grace.

> *whoever speaks, as one who utters oracles of God; whoever renders service, as one who renders it by the strength which God supplies; in order that in everything God may be glorified through Jesus Christ. To him belong glory and dominion forever and ever. Amen (1 Peter 4:11).*

How much of Jesus is in your life? Well, how much do you allow the grace of God to drive out the old man and take root in your heart, mind, soul, words, body, and in every other part of your being until only Jesus comes out? You will always find out what you have hidden in your heart when you're under pressure.

If you take a sponge and fill it with water, water comes out when you squeeze it. What comes out of you when you find yourself being pressed by the world? Is it the juice of grace or "woe is me"? If you are full of grace, the more you're pressured, the more grace will come out.

"I may be feeling bad *but...*"

"I may not have any money, *but…*"

"Someone broke into my house, *but…*

"All hell's coming against me, *but…*"

"*BUT…*God is for me, and if God is for me who can be against me? God is my defense! God is my king!"

Have doctors said you're going to die? Get your faith into action! Dispel the fear and say, "What's the worst thing that can happen? To die is gain. You just told me I'm going to be with Jesus soon." On the other hand, you then stand right up and say, "But… the Word of God says I shall live and not die!"

When my youngest daughter was fourteen years old she was thrown from a horse sustaining a severe brain injury. When the doctors told us she was dying, I said, "The <u>facts</u> are what we see, but the <u>truth</u> is what God's Word says!" and God's truth triumphed over the facts. She is here today, driving her car to work and she's going to be completely whole before Jesus comes.

This can only work by grace inside of you. When you have done all you can do, draw a line in the sand and say,

I will stand. I will stand victorious because I'm not standing in my strength; I am standing in the grace of God. There's nothing greater than the grace of God, the power of God, the holiness of God, and the Word of God! The Word is working in me. No weapon formed against me can prosper, and every word spoken against me shall be proven wrong because I am a servant of the Most High God. I will live by grace and faith, and I refuse to surrender to selfishness. I will not be moved by any other situation or circumstance. I will only be moved by the Word of the Living God!

It is impossible to be full of grace and not be happy. As I mentioned in a previous chapter, I used to be Eeyore. I went to bed being Eeyore, woke up being Eeyore, and even drank being Eeyore for many years. I had a perpetual cloud over my head and I assumed if it wasn't for bad luck, I had no luck at all. I went through my Eeyore period every three months and basically stayed depressed and discouraged.

When I was younger, I just didn't know what it meant to be happy. But when the Lord Jesus revealed His love to me, he filled me with grace and for the first time I really understood happiness. I stopped yielding to those destructive *Eeyore* feelings and began to yield to faith instead. I yielded to the Lord Jesus Christ, and grace has set me free!

"Happy are the people whose God is the Lord"
(Psalm 144:15).

You will find opportunities to not walk in grace every day. Some guy cuts you off, you say something dumb, your plans fall through, or someone hurts your feelings. I don't give in to negativity anymore because God's grace in me is far greater than any of those things. Now I can recognize things in myself that need to change, and I find something new every day. You know why? Because I *seek* grace every day. I've already discovered some things in myself that need to change today. By the time I get to heaven I will be completely transformed because there won't be anything of the old man left to argue with God anymore.

Surrendering the body is also an act of humility. Whether we realize it or not, our body can make a lot of demands on us. In fact, it likes to control us. The physical body is selfish without

Christ. It's all about self, and it wants pleasure for itself. Sometimes I hear Bluebell calling my name. The world may be stuck in this, but we are not.

As I allow the eternal Humble One to further seep into my being, this body becomes a greater living sacrifice, so that even my physical body can no longer control me. It can no longer dictate how I eat, how I do things, and it cannot demand anything for itself. I may live in a fallen body, but it is now dead to sin, and I realize my body no longer belongs to me. It belongs to Him.

> *"I appeal to you, therefore, brethren, by the mercies of God, to present your bodies as a living sacrifice, holy and acceptable to God, which is your spiritual worship"* *(Romans 12:1).*

Your body presented to the Lord is holy and acceptable to God. He loves your body as much as He loves your soul and your spirit, and He created a complete package. Redemption won't be fully complete until we have our glorified body, but right now the glorified body of Christ can live in this body, and the Spirit can so thoroughly possess me, that it will no longer yield to the lusts of the flesh. When you're full of grace, you won't sin. You can *choose* to sin and yield to the flesh, but you will miss the mark of God. We don't have to do this anymore! I can sow to the Spirit and reap life from the Spirit. I'm no longer controlled by my flesh, lust, and pride. As long as I will allow grace to work in me, I am free from sin. How can that which has died sin anymore?

Romans says the old you has died. I guarantee that if you go to a cemetery, you can't get one person out there to commit adultery. You can't get anyone out there to steal, kill, or lie. You can't get them do anything because they are dead! Paul is saying that as Christians, we are dead. The old man is gone, and therefore we are dead to sin. How can that which is born of God sin anymore and why in the world would you want to? Now, if you're selfish or self-centered or operating in pride, you will gravitate towards the flesh, but you do have a choice. Choose to be so full of grace your body becomes a living sacrifice.

"Do not be conformed to this world but be transformed by the renewal of your mind, that you may prove what is the will of God, what is good and acceptable and perfect" (Romans 12:2).

We have all been given a measure of faith and gifts have been placed on the inside of you, according to whatever part of the body God has called you to be.

For by the grace given to me I bid every one among you not to think of himself more highly than he ought to think, but to think with sober judgment, each according to the measure of faith which God has assigned him. For as in one body we have many members, and all the members do not have the same function, so we, though many, are one body in Christ, and individually members one of another. Having gifts that differ according to the grace given to us, let us use them (Romans 12:3-6).

We have the grace to heal the sick, raise the dead, and to cast out demons. We all carry the gifts of the Holy Spirit on the inside of us, but this verse is talking about specific parts of the church body. I'm called to be a head. If you're called to be a hand, are you *being* a hand? Are you a foot, or a heart, or a hidden part Paul says is even more important than what you can see? Are you being the specific part of the body of Christ He has called you to be?

If you have a gift of exhortation or encouragement, encourage people! If you have a gift of giving, give! If you have a gift of serving, serve! You may be called to be a hand or an arm or a leg, and you have been equipped with the grace to do that specific job. I don't have the grace to do what you do, and you don't have the grace to do what I do, and if we changed places, neither of us would likely be very successful. But if we stay within the grace given to us, it will bring mutual strengthening to the body of Christ because we have established ourselves in love by surrendering to the grace, and to Christ, our head, from whom every other part fits together. You can't just walk into a church and say, "Bless God, I'm going to be a _____ in your church! And if I don't get to be what I want, I'll go somewhere else until I find somebody who will listen to my flesh!"

You're God's temple. You've been purchased at an extraordinary price, and you don't belong to yourself anymore. Each one of you has a wonderful, remarkable grace inside of you.

For as in one body we have many members, and all the members do not have the same function, so we, though many, are one body in Christ, and individually members one of another" (Romans 12:4,5).

Your arms are part of your body. If you cut them off, those parts of your body are gone, and you won't be able to function properly. It takes all of us to make the body of Christ complete.

Having gifts that differ according to the grace given to us, let us use them: if prophecy, in proportion to our faith; if service, in our serving; he who teaches, in his teaching; he who exhorts, in his exhortation; he who contributes, in

liberality; he who gives aid, with zeal; he who does acts of
mercy, with cheerfulness (Romans 12:6-8).

As you yield, grace will become stronger in your life. If you have a desire in your heart to serve, serve. If it's from the Holy Spirit, you will abound from grace to grace to grace! Why would we withhold? We say things like,

"What about me?"

"What if I miss it?"

"Well, I don't want to do that."

"Well, I've never done that before..."

Some of you hold back because of stubbornness, and you carnally talk yourself out of the grace in you. Let's identify who is speaking here. If the grace is in you to do something and you resist it, you're listening to your old man.

I knew that I was called to be a minister from the time I was a boy, but I just did whatever I wanted to do for many years; still knowing the grace was in me to be a minister. I did everything I could to rebel against this grace, and the devil tried to kill me because I agreed with him. But when I surrendered to the call, the grace to be a pastor has been with me ever since, and it gets stronger and stronger because I embrace it. I invite grace to work through me.

"He who exhorts, in his exhortation; he who contributes, in
liberality" (Romans 12:8).

All of us are called to give, but there is a specific grace for some people to be paymasters in the body of Christ. They have the gift of giving. This says if you contribute, do it liberally. In other words, give yourself to the giving. God is not after your money; He's after *you!* Because when He has you, He has everything.

" Let he who gives aid, with zeal" (Romans 12:8).

Some of you love helping others. Do it with enthusiasm!

"...He who does acts of mercy, with cheerfulness" (Romans 12:8).

I was surprised the Lord said, "cheerfulness" there. But when you have the grace of mercy inside of you, you can be cheerful because you know that you're offering someone something they don't deserve. That's what mercy is about, therefore you must do it cheerfully -- and not give them mercy with a baseball bat. When you show mercy to someone who *knows* they don't deserve it, they're going to find grace, and they're going to get set free.

"And God is able to provide you with every blessing in abundance, so that you may always have enough of everything and may provide in abundance for every good work" (2 Corinthians 9:8).

CHAPTER TEN

FREEDOM IN CHRIST

IN 1986, I WAS SURPRISED to hear the Lord say, "*I want you to rent Mr. Roberts.*" It was a movie starring Henry Fonda, and it was about an officer on board a freighter ship. The captain was a bully and wouldn't allow the men to go on liberty. In the Navy, *liberty* means getting permission to leave the ship for some free time when you arrive in a port. The frustrated crew knew this was unfair and were getting ready to mutiny. Mr. Roberts finally convinced the captain to grant the men the liberty he was unfairly withholding, and the men were incredibly grateful to Mr. Roberts for obtaining their freedom.

When the Lord asked me to rent this movie, I thought, "Surely this can't be the Holy Spirit. He wouldn't tell me to rent a movie." So, I drove to the video store and rented a Disney movie for my daughters instead. When I got back home and opened the case, guess what was inside? It was *Mr. Roberts*! I said, "Well Lord, I guess you really do want me to watch it!"

As soon as it was over, the Lord told me that He would use me to bring liberty and freedom to the body of Christ. I believe this is true because God is so merciful and kind to me. Even now, He's still setting me free. If God can set me free, He can set you free. Christ has liberated all of us, and we can live in freedom because Jesus set us free!

I want to explore the freedom of Christ and shed some light on what this freedom entails. Christ purchased our liberty with His own blood. Now, we are a royal priesthood, a holy nation, and we are all priests unto God. We are the apple of His eye. We show forth His praises, His marvelous deeds, His majesty, and who He is.

Let's look at Paul's letter to the Galatians, who were Judaizers trying to influence the church to go back under the law. Paul's message to them basically said, "What is wrong with you? Have you lost your minds? Do you think the very thing which brought you into bondage will now bring you into freedom? Are you kidding? Freedom from the curse of the law can only be found in Christ!"

"For freedom Christ has set us free; stand fast therefore, and do not submit again to a yoke of slavery" (Galatians 5:1).

What is this freedom?

"For God so loved the world that He gave His only begotten Son that whosoever believes in Him should not perish, but have everlasting life" (John 3:16).

We miss so much in John 3:16! I believe I could teach on this verse until Jesus comes back and He would still reveal things we have never realized. If you think about it, you will understand that this single Scripture contains the entire Gospel. Freedom comes from the love of God, and the humility of Christ, so humility and love are the keys that unlock everything in the kingdom of God.

Humility is the Spirit of the kingdom of God, whereby self is dead, and the new man is alive unto God. I am free in Christ only because He humbled Himself. God sent His Son because He loved us, and Jesus emptied Himself of being equal with God when He came in human form. Think about it! The Son of God, God Himself, God the Son, *emptied Himself of being God* and chose to be born into this fallen flesh and die a terrible death. He destroyed sin in the flesh, destroyed the works of the devil, and His blood redeemed us.

Now, when we are born again, we experience something amazing because Jesus returned to the Father. We gradually empty ourselves of self. We empty ourselves of sin and of all that has fallen, to then be conformed to the image of God. God became a man so that man could become like God. Christ came as a man so that man can become like Christ. It all came from love, and it only works through humility.

> *"So faith, hope, love abide, these three; but the greatest of these is love" (1 Corinthians 13:13)*

We are the only people on earth who have the freedom to genuinely love others because we don't love them with a human love; it's an extraordinary kind of love. *Agape* is the love *of* God, and *from* God, whose very nature is love itself. Because I abide in this freedom, I can love you with the actual love of Christ.

I refuse to yield to the yoke of the slavery of sin, death, self, pride, Satan, or his dark kingdom anymore. I won't be subject to what other people think or say about me. Those forces come out of the kingdom of darkness, but Christ paid a tremendous price to obtain our freedom, and now I'm a new creation! I am free by the grace of God and the power of Christ in me, and I can now genuinely love with heaven's love, which is uncontaminated, unconditional, and unwavering.

We can love in the freedom of Christ, but only if self is dead. I'm talking about the old, unloving self. The one who says, "If you scratch my back, I'll scratch yours, and if you slap me, I'll slap you." Or, "I love you because I want something from you, so I'll act like your friend. I'm actually after something for myself, and I will get it at your expense."

That's the world talking. It's the flesh because the flesh is all about self. When self is out of the picture, you can freely operate in love and humility. Are you experiencing the freedom of Christ? You can always tell by surveying your actions.

It's not about, "Let's build a big church here!" Most churches are *gathering* churches. They reach out to gather to themselves, while a church operating in the freedom of Christ reaches out to the community with the love and power of Christ. Communities become God-conscious in response because the church is no longer *self*-conscious. We are to show the world we are a free people of another kingdom. In our kingdom, self is dead; it doesn't exist there.

We're so accustomed to self that we try to fit God's kingdom into it. We try to modify the kingdom of God, so it fits into man's doctrines and traditions, and into our opinions, and into who we think God is. We try to bring God down to our level and pull Him down to the bondage we're in, but Christ says, *"I'm bringing you out of bondage, and into the freedom only I can bring to you!"* We live in an ever-increasing kingdom which will endure forever. Jesus delivered us from slavery in a kingdom which will soon pass away, and we are no longer servants to sin or to fear.

Your greatest enemy is yourself, the old you. It's not the devil, because Jesus destroyed his works. Pride is the primary source of evil, and humility is entirely of God. Remember that our new man is humble. We are just like Jesus, the eternal Lamb of God, but our primary struggle is against the bondage of self.

"Look at me, Lord! Look at how good I am! Oh, you're going to be so happy when I get to heaven!"

He responds,

"I'm sorry, but the old man isn't welcome, so you're not coming. Your new man will be here, but no dead man can enter heaven. Only those who are alive unto God in Christ Jesus can enter in."

When you get to heaven, I believe many of you will be astounded when you fully realize who you are Christ. Self and pride are indisputably dead in heaven. Believers will make it into heaven, but humility will be a foreign concept to many of them, and they won't know themselves! They'll learn quickly though because there will be no resistance there from the old man. They'll be completely open to God. He can fast-forward you or microwave you there, but here on earth, He usually must slow cook the flesh out of us.

It's like you're in the oven looking out, and see the Master coming. You think, "Oh, good! He's going to let me out now!" He opens the door and looks at you, and says, *"Nope! You're not done yet,"* and then shuts the door again. He allows you to keep on cooking in the oven of grace and love. He's marinating you with His presence until the old man disappears, and you are filled with the aroma and flavor of Christ. He is cooking self out of you.

He destroyed self and brought us into freedom for Himself. We also have freedom from pride, freedom from sin, sickness, and disease. We are free from them all!

> *"For in Christ Jesus neither circumcision nor uncircumcision is of any avail, but faith working through love" (Galatians, 5:6).*

Love empowers faith. Paul said,

> *"And if I have prophetic powers, and understand all mysteries and all knowledge, and if I have all faith, so as to move mountains, but have not love, I am nothing" (1st Corinthians 13:2).*

If I have enough faith to move mountains, but I don't have love, it profits me nothing. A big old zip. Zero. But when I walk in the freedom and discipline of the kind of love which hems me in with Christ, then faith works to its highest potential because love is released to bless humanity with the power and presence of a loving God. Jesus said,

> *"For with the judgment you pronounce you will be judged, and the measure you give will be the measure you get" (Matthew 7:2).*

I really guard my heart against this. If I judge somebody with self-righteous judgment, the way I judge them will come right back to me. If you think this isn't true, check out your own life some time. Examine yourself, as Paul suggested. Think about times when you've judged somebody, and then recognize what has happened to you as a result. Paul said,

"Therefore let any one who thinks that he stands take heed lest he fall" (1 Corinthians 10:12).

The only person I care to judge is myself. How do I judge my old man? I reckon him dead, and therefore I stay in liberty. Christ has set me free, and liberty is love and humility.

Not one ounce of our flesh is welcome in the presence of God, but my new spirit holds everything that is good. All of God exists on the inside of me, and He wants to penetrate my soul, my mind, my thinking, my words, my actions, and even my body to keep it from sinning. This is freedom, and we can stand fast in it. How do we do it?

"For you were called to freedom, brethren; only do not use your freedom as an opportunity for the flesh, but by love serve one another" (Galatians 5:13).

We are free to choose good or evil. I can sow to the flesh, but I will reap from the flesh, which is death. I can also sow to the Spirit, and I will reap life, love, liberty, and freedom; for He is the Spirit of Freedom. He is merciful, loving, and kind. The Holy Spirit will never be satisfied with my life until I'm free.

The Holy Spirit is on this earth to substantiate the victory of Christ in the life of His people. He expresses the victory of Christ to a dying world through people who can heal the sick, raise the dead, cast out demons, and preach this wonderful gospel. We hold the key to everything the world needs, and what unlocks the keys of the kingdom are humility and love.

On the other hand, pride and self will always lock it. How do you know if you're operating in self? Just do a little self-examination.

Do you get angry at other people?

How much do other people irritate you?

How do you react when you don't get your way?

How do you respond when people don't embrace your greatest revelation?

People will be open to knowing Christ when they see Him in you. It's not *your* revelation they're looking for; it's the revelation of Jesus, and they need to see His nature and virtue in you. Do your words impart grace to the ears of the hearer, instead of dumb controversies which only cause people to argue?

Jesus purchased our freedom. Freedom to be like Him. Freedom to be ambassadors of God on earth to show them there is a greater kingdom. Freedom to live in this kingdom, but Paul warns us not to use it as an occasion for the flesh. This grace message is terrific, but it has been taken way too far, and some people say, "Oh, I can do anything I want to do. God is gracious, and He loves me ..." God does love you, but that's not what grace is about. Grace will discipline you and will make sure you don't sin.

Grace gives me the power to *not* sin. Grace gives me dominion over the forces of darkness. Grace gives me the liberty to live in the kingdom of God. I won't sin because of the grace of God in my life. I'm not going back to the bars or to being a mean and hateful person, because the grace of God is working in my life. Grace just won't let me go there anymore, and praise God, I have no desire to because I'm alive unto God in Christ Jesus. I am free in Christ now!

The next part of this verse says we are free to serve one another in love. The Scriptures can be summed up like this:

"You shall love your neighbor as yourself" (Mark 12:31).

"Love one another; even as I have loved you, that you also love one another" (John 13:34).

The Old Testament church couldn't love each other as Jesus loved them because they didn't have Christ. They were unable to love the way God loves because that kind of love just wasn't in them. However, they *could* love their neighbor as themselves.

In the New Covenant, Jesus instructed us to not only love our neighbor as ourselves but also to love them as He loved and gave Himself up for us as a sacrifice. We are also to sacrifice ourselves for others.

The greatest liberty is the ability to serve. Jesus came to serve, and not to be served. He served the world with the love of the Father, and we serve the world with the love of Christ and the Father. How often do we get caught up in ourselves and get mad when things don't go our way? If somebody says something we don't like, we get angry, and we live with our feelings on our sleeve. That's the old man, and it's bondage: not freedom.

When I put on the Lord Jesus Christ, I'm free to love you in the new man. It's all about love and humility. The old self can't do it, and pride is the food of self. Humility is the food of the new man, who is Christ in you because humility was His food. He ate the will of the Father, *(John 4:34)*, and became a sacrifice for us. We are to express the same sacrificial love towards other people.

If you're used to getting your way, that isn't freedom. In fact, when you always get your way, it only drives you deeper into the bondage of selfishness. Freedom comes as you continually walk in God's ways, begin to contemplate ways to bless people, and ask yourself questions like, "How do I release Christ to somebody? How do I help build somebody else up?"

Self-absorbed people believe church is about them. If only everyone were like them, the church wouldn't have any problems. When people think this way, *they* are the problem. Self is the reason people disappear when their noses get bent out of shape and then they choose not to love the body of Christ when people don't cater to them and treat them the way they think they should be treated. Self gets offended, but church, *we* are free!

We are free to give a kind of love the world doesn't know. We have a love that can bless the world if it spits in our face. If they curse us, we can pray for them. If they despitefully use us or if they hate us, we can do good to them in return. If they're our enemy, we can love them anyway. This is only possible when a dead man is walking, yet I'm alive unto God in Christ Jesus.

"Owe no man anything, except to love one another, for he who loves his neighbor has fulfilled the law" (Romans 13:8).

This verse tells us to owe no man anything except to love them, and not to be in debt to any man. I've known people who were entirely out of debt, and they were still meaner than snakes. If this verse were based on the principle that you could love people as soon as you are out of financial debt, then you would only be doing it as a badge of pride. I know other people who are struggling and deeply in debt, but they're filled with such a love of God. God wants us free!

I was a mean person before I was born again. I was full of anger and bitterness and resentment, and I hated people. I was a mess and a candidate for hell. But God said, *"I'm not going to let you go there, I've got a better life for you."*

When I committed myself back to Jesus, He grounded me in

love, which was the very opposite of who I was. He spoke to me of love and molded me in love, and I allowed love to mold me. Why? Because everything in the old Rich Van Winkle hammered the nails in His hands and stuck the sword in His side. I pressed the thorns on His head. I laid the stripes on His back. I bruised Him, and I crucified Him. I refuse to do that anymore, and only the grace of love and the freedom of Christ can prevent me from doing it again. Now I am a new creation.

I don't share this very often, but I had a visitation in heaven. I was standing there with everyone, and then Jesus entered the room. I heard a voice say,

"Behold the Lamb of God, who took away the sin the world!"

Then they referred to His precious blood. When they said the word "blood," everyone in heaven fell on their face. It was so reverent and holy. I just dropped, fearful and trembling... and grateful.

By the grace of God, I choose to never to profane the Blood of Christ by my actions or my words towards another human being because Christ shed His precious blood for them. I don't care how vile they are, how backslidden they are, or how unsaved they are; it doesn't matter. Jesus shed His blood for that person, and I have no control over whether they receive the gift or not. That is their choice, but I do have control over the way I treat them.

If we can't wash the feet of the very least of God's people, then we're not walking in love. We usually don't mind washing the feet of the mature people. They're in church, and they're respectable and happy, and they're great people; but what about those who are weak? What about those who are a mess, or those who just don't seem to get it? How willing are we to wash *their* feet as one of Christ's very own? It's easy to wash the feet of a saint, but what about the ones who don't act very saintly?

Jesus washed the feet of Judas Iscariot, the very one He knew would betray Him. If God washed the feet of men, how much more then, should we? It's not about physical washing; it's about washing the dirt off to be able to touch that person with the love of Christ and to serve them.

We were purchased to be free, and our freedom gives us the ability to serve and wash the feet of others. Therefore, Paul said to stand in this freedom.

> *"Don't yield again to the yoke of the bondage of the flesh and the curse of the law" (Galatians 5:1).*

Don't yield to those things but serve out of love as Jesus did. Jesus came and emptied Himself, so we were obtained through love and humility. God's grace and the freedom of Christ enable us to live in love and humility.

God is seeking people through which He can love the world, with signs and wonders and miracles far beyond anything we have ever seen! The kingdom of God is His manifested presence, and in His presence, there is healing, salvation, wholeness, and deliverance. I believe the Holy Spirit is searching hearts, looking for those who have humbled themselves.

Flesh is easy to identify. If you are carrying around hurt feelings, you haven't humbled yourself. If you haven't forgiven, you don't understand what Christ did for you. If you know *you* are forgiven by the Most High God, why in the world would you not forgive a brother or sister? What do you think about? What are you mad about? Who are you upset with? What has anyone done to you that is more powerful than the cross?

Don't magnify the loss instead of the cross. Choose to

magnify the cross because God has set you free! He poured out the blood of His Son for you. He tortured and turned is back on His Son on the cross, and it pleased Him to do it because of His great love for us.

Jesus humbled Himself to go to that cross because of His immeasurable love for us, so we could also come to the Father. How much more then should we show this kind of love to others? We can *only* do this through the freedom Christ purchased with His own blood. Furthermore, we can't bring a brother or sister out of bondage if we are not free, ourselves. All of us are growing, and the more freedom we have in Christ, the more we can set others free.

Sometimes we don't thank God enough for what He's done for us, what He's doing for us now, and for what He will do forever. Someday the kingdom of God will rule and will drive out the kingdom of pride, but it must start in our hearts. I have a little round rug at my house. Sometimes I stand in the middle of it, point to my heart, and say, "Lord, right here. Let's start right here. I can't do anything without you."

Do you want freedom? Do you believe it's the perfect will of God for you? What's stopping you? Look in the mirror say, "Jesus, I am not going to stop you anymore!" Then you will walk in the freedom and liberty of the new man, and you'll never again wonder if God is mad at you or not. When you have done something wrong, you will know how much love He has for you. Love and humility set us free, and love and humility keep us free.

CHAPTER ELEVEN

OUR IDENTITY IN CHRIST

WE ARE STEADILY BECOMING the image of Jesus, both inwardly and outwardly, as His body. Jesus is beautiful. I wish we could see Him as John did. His eyes were full of light and fire and glory and power and love. That's the way He is, and it's also the way we are because we are the body of Christ.

Our body connects to our head. Our brain sends signals to our heart, directing it to beat. It tells the muscles to move, and the lungs to breathe. Everything that flows through our body comes from our head. The body responds to the head, and what is in the head gives life to the body. Some folks might ask, "Doesn't my heart keep me alive?" Yes, it does, but it would stop pumping if your brain stopped working.

When someone's brain is damaged, it affects the body. Strokes or head injuries can cause parts of the body not to function correctly because a part of the brain is damaged.

However, Jesus does not have brain damage. His infinitely sharp mind holds the universe together. We also have the mind of Christ, and the whole body joins together through Him.

But Jesus beholds us as so much more than we can conceive of, consider or imagine. I want to share something He recently said to me. It was so beautiful that I wrote it down.

To my Beautiful Bride,

I love you! I nurture you. You are the love of my life, the glory of our Father. My Spirit is preparing you for myself. Though you suffer on earth, it is preparing you for a greater weight of glory. I bought you for my Father with my own life, and now you are the dwelling place of my Spirit; the Father's gift to you. My covenant love for you is forever. I am jealous over you with an everlasting love.

Oh, how much He loves us! When we were born again, we became a vital part of His body. We were sealed by His Spirit and purchased by His blood through the love of God, our Father. That's how much God loves us, and Jesus has fallen in love with us, with an everlasting love.

A sign of spiritual maturity is the degree to which we respond to His love and return it back to Him. He loves each one of us as much as another. He even loves the lost, and desires that *none* should perish. How much do we love Him back?

We will undoubtedly reflect the one we're in love with, and if we're more in love with the world, it's going to show in our thoughts and our actions. We have the incredible love of Christ, (our head), which fills us, (His body), with Himself. Jesus said,

> *Abide in me, and I in you. As the branch cannot bear fruit by itself, unless it abides in the vine, neither can you, unless you abide in me. I am the vine, you are the branches. He who abides in me, and I in him, he it is that bears much fruit, for apart from me you can do nothing. If a man does not abide in me, he is cast forth as a branch and withers; and the branches are gathered, thrown into the fire and burned. If you abide in me, and my words abide in you, ask whatever you will, and it shall be done for you. By this my Father is glorified, that you bear much fruit, and so prove to be my disciples. As the Father has loved me, so have I loved you; abide in my love. If you keep my commandments, you will abide in my love, just as I have kept my Father's commandments and abide in his love. These things I have spoken to you, that my joy may be in you, and that your joy may be full. "This is my commandment, that you love one another as I have loved you (John 15:4-12).*

Love is the fulfillment of the law, and the Holy Spirit has shed the love of God abroad in our hearts, so He has given us the ability to love. The love of Christ is in us, which is also the love of the Father. The Father loves us with the very same love He loves Jesus with, and we're to abide in that love. This means I am to love you with that kind of love; just as Jesus loves you and gave Himself up for you. We have supernatural grace on the inside of us to do this because we are being transformed into His image. We are His reflection, and we are just as He is.

The glory of God is in us forever and ever. The Lord wants

the world to see Him in us and experience Him through us because we are the only ones on the earth who can preach the good news of Jesus Christ. We have the Word of Grace on the inside of us. We also have the great grace of God, and it's not about being perfect; it's about our willingness to be perfected. God will have His way in our life because He said,

"He who calls you is faithful, and he will do it" (1 Thessalonians 5:24).

We only need to allow Him to do it, and this comes from obedience, humility, faith, and trusting Him with all our heart. There must be a deep cry within us, saying, "Lord don't let me do anything that would hurt your heart and not reflect you." I believe that out of a sincere desire of our heart, God will be faithful -- and Christ will be faithful to fill us with Himself.

If you look at yourself in the mirror, you might see some blemishes, but He will remove them. He has come to take every spot, wrinkle or blemish out of us, His church. It isn't our responsibility to point out the blemishes and iron the wrinkles out of the body of Christ; that's His job.

Some misguided Christians seem to think they have the "Spirit of an Iron," and it's their calling to iron the wrinkles out and straighten out folks in the church. That's not anyone's calling in the body of Christ, and it's all about self. I guess there's no nice way to say "self-righteous."

Speaking the truth doesn't mean just getting it off our chest; He instructed us to, "speak the truth in *love.*" We're growing up in Christ, and we are becoming like Him. We are living in truth, walking in truth, and speaking the truth; which is speaking and living in love. When we are saved, we start out as new (baby) Christians. As we grow, we become more and more like Christ because we are steadily being filled with Him on the inside, and we increasingly reflect who He is on the outside.

As we allow the Word of God and the Spirit of God to cultivate who we are, we gradually begin to reflect Him, and we will find ourselves living as He did. We don't have any fear, because perfect love casts out all fear (1 John 4:18). God will always take care of you, no matter what your life looks like, or how bad it seems. He is far greater than anything that looks impossible to you. It doesn't get much worse than realizing the Egyptian army is behind you and the Red Sea is in front of you, and you're about to be destroyed by the greatest military force in the world. But God...

But God... He knew all along which path the Israelites would take. Nothing surprises God. He didn't sit up there and say, *"Well Son, what are we going to do now? They're sure in a pickle down there."* No, He said, *"I brought them to this very place to show them my greatness!"* and then He parted the Red Sea! If God can part the Red Sea, is there anything in your life too difficult for Him? Is *anything* too difficult? All things are possible for those who believe.

Ephesians 4:15-16 refers to the body of Christ and shows us how we are meant to function.

> *Rather, speaking the truth in love, we are to grow up in every way into him who is the head, into Christ, from whom the whole body, joined and knit together by every joint with which it is supplied, when each part is working properly, makes bodily growth and upbuilds itself in love"* (Ephesians 4:15,16).

We can disconnect if we choose to remain carnal Christians. This can happen through our thoughts, words, or our actions, but nothing will ever change the fact that we will always belong to His body. I don't know about you, but I have disengaged many times, and if you had been there you would have had no idea I had ever met Jesus.

People detach. This doesn't mean that we are no longer part of His body, but we can become a non-functioning part whenever we feel self-righteous or condemned because of our own actions. Sin naturally causes us to feel detached from Him, but nothing can separate us from the love of God in Christ Jesus (Romans 8:39), so there's never a real separation: only a lack of faith.

If we move into in this area, we can beat ourselves up and then end up feeling discouraged, depressed, and damaged. At this point, many people backslide and even leave the church. Although we may do some dumb things, we will always be a necessary part of His body. We may *feel* disconnected, but this will never be the case because Jesus will always try to reconnect us with Himself. We don't realize He's up there saying,

> *Hey, come back! I'm right here. I love you, and I'm not going anywhere. Hey! I forgive you. Let's reconnect. Let me bring grace and love and happiness back into your heart. I can fix it. Let me fill you with myself. Come back... I love you!*

Jesus is always waiting for us to come back. Who can ever separate us from the love of God in Christ Jesus? Nobody! No height, no depth, no demons, no principalities...

If my right arm decided it didn't want to be a part of my body and it took off to do its own thing, it would still be part of my body, and I would always want it back. I don't know about you, but I need to have hands and feet and elbows and knees and internal organs and eyes and ears and everything else functioning normally to be complete. I don't want to lose even one part of my body, and neither does the Lord Jesus Christ. He wants every part of His body functioning and healthy.

Countless things can cause us to disengage and keep us from being effective if we let them, but no matter what, your body will always be your body. Throughout my life, I have discovered that His love for me will always be greater than anything I could ever do, and He will still be waiting for me to run back to Him. You know why? Because He's my head, and I will always, always be a necessary part of His body. As the body of Christ, we go from glory to glory, faith to faith, and from strength to strength.

We all say and do dumb things. Thankfully, Jesus will always be bigger than our mistakes. He will still be in us and will never leave us or forsake us. He's not a conditional God who will be there when we're good but then abandon us when we're bad. Jesus will always be there, no matter what. He will be *in* us and *with* us forever.

Our physical body changes as we age. It may not be as strong and healthy as it used to be, and you may not think it's as attractive as it once was, but it's still your body. As our physical body ages and slows down, just the opposite happens on a spiritual level. God catches us and does a reverse process in us. As we age on a physical level, we become younger and healthier in the spirit; and someday our spiritual body will be fully connected to His.

He saves us in whatever condition we're in and starts working Himself in us, so we increasingly become more and more like Him. When He came and got me, I was struggling with alcoholism. I was a drunk and a fighter and a mess, but Jesus came to clean up messes! He did *not* come and say, *"Well, you know as soon as you perfect yourself, I'll come save you."* There was no way I could perfect myself, but praise God, He came and saved me anyway, and He said, *"We are now and forever part of each other."*

Most of us have been deeply and unfairly wounded by others. Unfortunately, this is just part of being on this earth, but you should not let it define you. Instead, accept your identity in Christ, and all that He has said about you. Bask in His deep and unfailing love for you and focus on everything He has done on your behalf. Allow Him to define your life, and the hurtful words and negative things you have experienced will break off you, so you will be free to love.

I'm not here to make you into the image of Christ; the Holy Spirit began this transformation the moment you were saved. God has said many wonderful things about you are in Christ. You are His body, His church, His identical twin, His friend, His beloved bride, and so much more.

I knew a pastor many years ago who probably walked in more love than any man I've ever met. He dismissed one particular service by saying, "I want you to say three words to somebody in this room. Hug them and say, 'I love you.'" One man happened to be experiencing a severe heart attack at the time, and the first person who hugged him said, "I love you, brother." He was healed instantly, and he came up afterward to give his testimony. You are becoming more and more like Jesus every day. Consider saying those three words to somebody who isn't expecting it this week. You may never know how it will impact their life.

As we learn to walk in faith, humility, love, and grace, we will steadily become more and more like Christ in every way. God said, *"I will make them in my image and likeness"* and so here we are, created to be like Him. The Holy Spirit started a beautiful transformation process the very moment we became born-again.

"For those whom he foreknew he also predestined to be conformed to the image of his Son, in order that he might be

the firstborn among many brethren"(Romans 8:29).

So, Jesus is the firstborn among many brethren, and we are being transformed into His very image, His identical twin. He sincerely desires to have a body and a people who are just like Him. That's us!

God not only sent His only begotten Son on our behalf, but He also sent the Holy Spirit, His Word, and sufficient grace to overcome sin and self, which enables us to embrace the endless, excellent work that is going on inside of us.

"In this is love perfected with us, that we may have confidence for the day of judgment, because as he is so are we in this world" (1 John 4:17).

CHAPTER TWELVE

HOW TO MEDITATE ON THE
WORD OF GOD

G OD WANTS YOU TO PROSPER and be successful. He has never set anybody up to fail except the heathens and the lost and the devil. Once you're born again, you are set up for success! God gave you the Word to sow into your heart so that you can be prosperous.

> *This Book of the Law shall not depart out of your mouth, but you shall meditate on it day and night, that you may be careful to do according to all that is written in it; for then you shall make your way prosperous, and then you shall have good success (Joshua 1:8).*

This is the only time in the Bible you'll find the word "success." How do you become prosperous and successful in the things of God, in your business, in your life, and in your ministry? Meditate on the Word of God.

When we meditate on the Word, rest assured the Word will come out of our heart. To meditate on something means to focus your thoughts on it, reflect on it, and ponder it. In other words, to dwell on it. A lot of people think they don't have enough time to meditate, but we all have more control over our time and our thoughts than we may realize, and we all make time for our priorities.

I understand that you may have a demanding job, but you still have authority over the rest of your time. What are you planting in your heart then? "Well, I've been working so hard, and I need to relax and do things I enjoy." If you're substituting those things for spending time with God and in His Word, you're only spinning your wheels and missing out on more than you can imagine. The Word of God abiding in you will give you refreshment, encouragement, strength, and wisdom. The benefits are almost endless. David said,

> *"Let the Words of my mouth and the meditation of my heart be acceptable in thy sight, O Lord, my rock and my redeemer" (Psalm 19:14).*

Whatever you are meditating on will be obvious; just take note of what you are talking about. Your words and the meditation of your heart are always tied together.

> *"The good person out of the good treasure of his heart produces good, and the evil person out of his evil treasure produces evil, for out of the abundance of the heart his mouth speaks" (Luke 6:45).*

So how do you meditate on the Word of God? Smith

Wigglesworth was an evangelist who taught the Word with great revelation. One story relates that a Greek and a Hebrew scholar approached him after one of his meetings to ask where he got such revelation. He replied, "Some people like to read their Bible in the Hebrew; some like to read it in the Greek; I like to read it in the Holy Spirit!" Wigglesworth would read a Scripture, and then he would pray in tongues. He would reread the Scripture, and then he would pray in tongues again. Then he would repeat this process.

When I was baptized in the Holy Spirit and began to understand it is the meditation of my heart which empowers this Word to work in my life, I would read the Bible and then put it on my head and walk around praying in tongues. Then I would put it over my heart and pray in tongues. Then I'd put it back on my head and pray in tongues again because I realized that whatever I put in my heart will begin to affect what I'm thinking. I would do this for hours. I'm sure if anyone had seen me they would have thought I was crazy, but I wasn't. I was saying, "God, I'm going to hide your Word in my heart. Holy Spirit, I'm going to pray in tongues because you're the one who empowers this." I would do it over and over because of my love for this Word.

You may think, "Well, that's good for you, Pastor. You have lots of time to read." I do, and I'm grateful for a calling which allows me to do it, but I use my time wisely. I love spending time with the Lord. I would do it, anyway, but I'm thankful I can. However, when I wasn't pastoring, I was no stranger to hard work. I ran a jackhammer and broke up concrete, and its backbreaking work. We were given a 15-minute break, and I used that time to meditate on a Scripture I had previously written down. Then on my half-hour lunch break, I would go off by myself and meditate on it some more. When I went to the bathroom, I would sit down and do the same thing. There many ways to reflect on the Word, and no matter what your schedule looks like, you can squeeze in times during the day to meditate on a Scripture.

If your schedule looks anything like mine did, let me encourage you to pick out a Scripture to meditate on, write it down and take it with you. Find a quiet place during your break and read it, instead of going into the break room where everybody's complaining about something or another. Study the Scripture and talk to the Holy Ghost.

Have you ever heard of cows chewing their cud? Cows have four stomachs. First, they eat and eat and fill their first stomach, and then they regurgitate the food and chew on it awhile. They chew on it until it's broken down and then it goes into the second stomach, and it follows this process until it finally gets down into the fourth stomach and produces milk.

Meditation works the same way. Take the Word and regurgitate it into your thinking until your heart is receiving and processing it. Your heart will ensure that it grows. If you're spending more time meditating on the news and the matters of the world, the world will increase in your heart because it is no respecter of the seeds you put in it. This is the way it works.

One of the most foolish things a person can do is view this Word as merely paper and ink and entirely miss the fact that it is Christ Himself, the Living Word. This Bible is altogether about Him. The Holy Spirit, who authored this book, revealed this to me as I sat with Him, meditating and listening and telling Jesus and the Father and the Holy Spirit how much I love them.

Sometimes I'll read a Scripture, and even feel compelled to kiss it. It's like having Jesus right there with me. There have been times I have lain my head on my Bible, and it was like putting my head on His chest and loving Him. Sometimes it gets so intense I find myself weeping because of the depth I find there. I love God's Word, and it is alive.

Where I am today has absolutely nothing to do with Rich Van Winkle, but everything to do with the Word of God and His grace. They work in partnership to make me more like Jesus, and God is no respecter of persons. I have been meditating on this Word for many years now, but if I get away from it for any length of time, I'll start feeling and acting miserable. Just ask my wife. She can tell if I've been taking in the Word or not because I'm a mess without it. If I ever stop making it a priority and start planting seeds of the world back into my heart, I will backslide, and will inevitably be pulled back under the control of the flesh.

I know a lot of Christians who dearly love God but allowed somebody to hurt their feelings, or didn't get their way about something, and they backslid. They planted doubt and negativity into their heart, and the Word was choked out of their hearts and became unfruitful in their lives.

The Word of Grace builds us up and strengthens us, but it can only work in your life if you keep planting it in your heart and germinating it through humility and meditation. That's the power of the Word of God working in you through the Holy Spirit. The more of the Word you put in your heart, and the more you meditate on it and obey it, the more you will find yourself changing. Your thinking will change, the way you say things will change, and the way you see things will change because you'll see them in the light of God's Word. Then, success and prosperity will follow.

You know, God has been in a killing process in my life. He has killed the old man and put him on the cross where he belongs and replaced him with the Word of God. How long will the entire process take? I don't know; it's not my problem. My job is to keep putting the Word in my heart and keep meditating on it. Whatever you hide in your heart will produce the fruit you will live with because it grows out of whatever is in your heart.

"Death and life are in the power of the tongue, and those who love it will eat its fruits" (Proverbs 18:21).

Some of us would undoubtedly profit from putting duct tape over our mouths and just stop talking until we have meditated on the Word enough to only speak faith. If you took a tape recorder with you every morning and then listened to it before going to bed, you would find out what kind of fruit is in your heart by listening to what you've been saying all day.

I would rather spend time with the Lord and meditate on this Word than do anything else, but God has called me to do other things. I've not been called to a monastery; I'm married. I love being married and will always want to be married. I love my family, and I love ministering, but my first and greatest love is the Word of Grace because it's the way Jesus makes me more like Himself.

If you happen to be feeling a little behind in your reading and meditating right now, keep in mind that you can't run a marathon right off the bat. You may be thinking, "Oh my gosh, I've got so much catching up to do!" No, relax and start wherever you are. Sit down with the Word and the Holy Spirit and say, "Lord, I'm going to meditate on this Word." Let it soak deep down inside of you. Don't just do a five-minute morning devotion, feel good about yourself, and go about your day, because that seed will be snatched out of your heart quickly and will never conform you to the image of Christ. If you haven't been meditating on the Word, now is a great time start. If you have been doing it, praise God, keep on going!

God is searching for people who have more of His Word in their hearts than the word of the world. The Holy Spirit is instructing His church to hide the Word in our hearts because the days we live in are evil. Worldly thinking cannot impart life to you and can hurt you. God will never agree with your opinions, so you might as well humble yourself and say, "Lord, give me wisdom and knowledge through Your Word." As a result, you will become the person He has called you to be, walking in His grace and you will be successful and prosper in everything He calls you to do.

MY PRAYER FOR YOU

Father, thank you for conforming us to the image and likeness of your Son, Jesus, by the power of the Word and the Spirit of Grace. I can't thank you enough for brothers and sisters, and that we are a family. Jesus, you are our elder brother, and we're your identical twins. Father, there's no way to thank you for all Jesus has done except to give you a surrendered life to glorify His name. Lord, show each person the magnitude of freedom you purchased for them and give them the grace to walk in perfect freedom, so your love can flow through them to the world. Holy Spirit, I pray that you would touch the heart of every person reading this, so they will accept the grace and humility to become more and more like You every day. May the glory of the Lord rest upon them so they will be a light to the body of Christ, unto the nations, and to the cities. I release this over your people. It's in your Word, and it's your will. May your will be done in your kingdom, and may it be done in our lives, on earth as well as in heaven. In Jesus' Precious and Holy Name. Amen.

ACKNOWLEDGEMENTS

" May the LORD repay you for your kindness, and may
your reward be full from the LORD, the God of Israel."
Ruth 2:12 (Amp)

I would first like to thank God for His Son, His Word, His Spirit, His grace, and His infinite love and guidance in supplying the knowledge and direction for this endeavor.

Many thanks to Darlene Trowbridge for transcribing and editing my sermons and for her idea of putting this book together. Nick Loy, your insight, suggestions, and attention to detail have been invaluable. Chris O'Chenski, thank you for sharing your talents on the cover photograph and design, as well as for your efforts in coordinating the details to make this cover possible. Justin Van Winkle, I could not be happier to have my son's picture on the cover. Debbie Brown, David Trowbridge and Mike Bauman, your suggestions and input have also been greatly appreciated.

I would also like to express my sincerest gratitude to Bruce Marchiano and *Marchiano Ministries* for so generously allowing us to use his image as Jesus in the mirror. And last but not least, thank you, Joe Ewen, for volunteering to write the foreword, and for everything you wrote. Your friendship has always been a tremendous blessing.

43637286R00078

Printed in Poland
by Amazon Fulfillment
Poland Sp. z o.o., Wrocław